THE CHATEAUX OF
FRANCE

COUNTRY LIFE

THE CHATEAUX OF
FRANCE

⚜

PHOTOGRAPHS *BY* FREDERICK H. EVANS

FROM THE ARCHIVES *OF* COUNTRY LIFE

1897 - 1939

MARCUS BINNEY

MITCHELL BEAZLEY

For Anne, my wife.

First published in Great Britain 1994 by Mitchell Beazley
an imprint of Reed Consumer Books Limited
Michelin House, 81 Fulham Road, London SW3 6RB
and Auckland, Melbourne, Singapore and Toronto

Executive Art Editor: Larraine Shamwana
Design: Carroll Associates
Editor: John Wainwright
Production: Heather O'Connoll

Art Director: Jacqui Small
Executive Editor: Judith More

A CIP record for this book is available from the British Library

ISBN 1 85732 531 1

Produced by Mandarin Offset
Printed and bound in China

Front endpaper: Valençay
Title page: Châteaudun
Rear endpaper: La Rochefoucauld

FRENCH CHÂTEAUX
PHOTOGRAPHED
BY FREDERICK EVANS
1906-7

Locations and year photographed given where known.
*Asterisk denotes châteaux that appear in this book.

ANET EURE-ET-LOIR *1906*
ANGERS MAINE-ET-LOIRE
*ANTERROCHES CANTAL *1907*
AUNEAU EURE-ET-LOIR *1907*
AVRILLY ALLIER
AZAY-LE-RIDEAU INDRE-ET-LOIRE *1906*
BALLEROY CALVADOS *1906*
*LA BASTIE D'URFÉ LOIRE
BEAUCAIRE GARD
BEAUMESNIL EURE *1907*
*BLOIS LOIR-ET-CHER *1906*
LE BOIS DE MOUTIERS SEINE-MARITIME
BOISY LOIRE
BOISCORNILLÉ ILE-ET-VILAINE *1906*
BONNELLES SEINE-ET-OISE *1906*
BONNÉTABLE SARTHE *1907*
BOUMOIS MAINE-ET-LOIRE *1907*
*BOURSAULT MARNE
*LA BRÈDE GIRONDE *1907*
CARCASSONNE AUDE *1907*
*CHAMBORD LOIR-ET-CHER *1906*
CHAMPS SEINE-ET-MARNE *1907*
CHANTILLY OISE *1906*
*CHASTELLUX YONNE
*CHÂTEAUDUN EURE-ET-LOIR *1907*
*CHÂTEAU-GAILLARD EURE
*CHAUMONT LOIR ET-CHER
*CHAUMONT LA GUICHE SAONE-ET-LOIRE

*CHEMAZÉ (Saint-Ouen) MAYENNE *1907*
CHENONCEAU INDRE-ET-LOIRE
CHEVENON NIÈVRE
*CHEVERNY LOIR-ET-CHER *1906*
CHINON INDRE-ET-LOIRE
CINQ MARS INDRE-ET-LOIRE *1906*
CLERMONT LOIRE-ATLANTIQUE
COULAINE INDRE-ET-LOIRE *1907*
*COURTANVAUX SARTHE *1907*
COUZIERS INDRE-ET-LOIRE *1906*
CREULLY CALVADOS
*ERMENONVILLE OISE
*ESCLIMONT EURE-ET-LOIR
*EU SEINE-MARITIME *1906*
FALAISE CALVADOS
FÉNELON DORDOGNE
FONTAINE-HENRY CALVADOS *1906*
LA GASCHERIE LOIRE-ATLANTIQUE *1907*
*LA GRANGEFORT PUY-DE-DOME
GROSBOIS VAL-DE-MARNE *1907*
*HAUTEFORT DORDOGNE *1907*
JOSSELIN MORBIHAN
KERJEAN FINISTÈRE
*LANDIFER MAINE-ET-LOIRE
LANGEAIS INDRE-ET-LOIRE
LION-SUR-MER CALVADOS *1906*
LOCHES INDRE-ET-LOIRE *1906*
*LONRAI ORNE *1907*
LE LUDE SARTHE
LUYNES INDRE-ET-LOIRE
*MAINTENON EURE-ET-LOIR *1907*
*MEILLANT CHER
MEMILLION *1907*
*MONTIGNY-LE-GANELON EURE-ET-LOIR *1907*
MONTMELAS RHONE
MONTRÉSOR INDRE-ET-LOIRE *1906*
*MONTREUIL-BELLAY MAINE-ET-

LOIRE
MONTSABERT MAINE-ET-LOIRE *1907*
MOREUIL SOMME
LA MOTTE-GLAIN LOIRE-ATLANTIQUE
LE MOULIN LOIR-ET-CHER *1907*
*NANTES LOIRE-ATLANTIQUE
O ORNE *1906*
LA PALICE (LAPALISSE)
LE PERCHER MAINE-ET-LOIRE *1907*
*PIERREFONDS OISE *1906*
RAMBURES SOMME *1906*
RÉAUX INDRE-ET-LOIRE *1907*
*LA ROCHEFOUCAULD CHARENTE
LES ROCHERS DE SEVIGNÉ ILE-ET-VILAINE
*LE ROCHERS-MÉZANGERS MAYENNE *1907*
DE ROZAY *1907*
SAINT-AIGNAN LOIR-ET-CHER *1906*
SAINT-AGIL LOIR-ET-CHER *1907*
SAINT-FARGEAU YONNE
SANSAC INDRE-ET-LOIRE *1906*
SAUMUR MAINE-ET-LOIRE *1907*
SERRANT MAINE-ET-LOIRE *1907*
SUCY-EN-BRIE VAL-DE-MARNE
SULLY-SUR-LOIRE LOIRET *1907*
TANCARVILLE SEINE-MARITIME
TARASCON BOUCHES-DU-RHONE
DE TILLY SEINE-ET-OISE *1907*
USSÉ INDRE-ET-LOIRE *1906*
*VALENÇAY INDRE
*VALLIÈRE OISE *1906*
*VAUX-LE-VICOMTE SEINE-ET-MARNE *1906*
*VERVAINE ORNE
VIGNY SEINE-ET-OISE *1906*
VILLEBON EURE-ET-LOIR *1907*
VITRÉ ILE-ET-VILAINE *1906*
VRAINVILLE *1907*

CONTENTS

In 1906 the photographer Frederick Evans set off for France with a bicycle and a roving commission to photograph châteaux for *Country Life*. Over the next eighteen months or so he visited and recorded one hundred châteaux, as well as cathedrals, parish churches and historic town houses. A selection of the châteaux appeared in *Country Life*'s weekly country-house slot over the next fifteen years, and most of these were republished in 1916 in a sumptuous folio volume, *Twenty Five Great Houses of France*, with a text by Sir Theodore Andrea Cook. Yet of Evans's remarkable cache of one hundred châteaux no more than half were ever published in *Country Life*. The remainder slumbered as negatives in the magazine's archive, unseen and virtually forgotten (though Evans evidently made presentation prints of a few of them for exhibitions and as presents to friends, and these appear occasionally in auction catalogues).

When I began work on this book the main châteaux were already well-known. Among these were Richard Cœur de Lion's Château Gaillard, and mighty Pierrefonds, restored by Viollet-le-Duc. The famous Loire châteaux were also there: Amboise and Chaumont, Blois and Chambord, Azay-le-Rideau and Chenonceau. The main omission was Villandry – hardly surprising as it was only in 1906 that Dr Joachim Carvallo and his American wife bought the château and embarked on the creation of its extraordinary gardens.

There was no original correspondence or documentation to go with the photographs – only the names of the châteaux inscribed on the negative sleeves and sometimes on the negatives themselves. However, this information had been recently gathered together in an excellent typescript catalogue by Paulette Barton. Scanning the list of châteaux photographed by Evans I was surprised how many were unfamiliar to me. For nearly fifteen years I had also been going to France to photograph châteaux for *Country Life* articles with the magazine's staff photographer Alex Starkey, and had been constantly on the lookout for beautiful, impressive but little-known examples. Evans, however, working apparently on his own initiative, had struck an extraordinarily rich seam.

Evans was particularly strong on Medieval and Renaissance châteaux, and the 17th century was well represented too – reflecting the interest during the early years of this century in Inigo Jones, Sir Christopher Wren and their contemporaries. Only on the 18th century was he weak, though this was hardly surprising given the taste of the time. But with the 19th century came an unexpected surge: namely, a large number of richly painted Gothic-Revival interiors, and a whole series of substantial châteaux in revivalist style, some evidently completed little more than ten years before Evans arrived in France.

However, the richest seam of all lay in patrician houses of no particular date which had grown over the centuries – houses steeped in history and atmosphere, but not by any sense in the first rank of historic houses an English

Montrésor

visitor would set out to see. This is partly explained by the fact that while Evans, during his first year in France, in 1906, had worked principally in the 'obvious' places – Normandy, the Ile-de-France and the Loire valley – in 1907 he had travelled much further afield: to Champagne in the east, to Gascony and the Auvergne, to Toulouse and Tarascon in the south.

Apart from the actual names of the châteaux I had neither the names of owners, nor any hint of a location – not an address, a nearby town nor a department. I thus worked my way carefully through the twelve beautifully illustrated *Merveilles des Châteaux*, published by Réalités and Hachette, covering France region by region. (Each volume features thirty to forty châteaux and provides a short paragraph at the back on a further two to four hundred, thereby covering nearly four thousand châteaux in all. Even so, I was left with thirty châteaux that were still unidentified.

Fortunately, it was at this point that a French friend told me of a library at Creteil, outside Paris, which had an *Annuaire des Châteaux* for the years 1889-90, 1917-18 and 1920-21. I tracked it down in the British Library, but when it arrived on my desk I had a shock: the châteaux were listed under owners and there were as many names as you would find in a telephone directory. (I later read that 40,000 château owners were listed in the 1888 Annuaire.) Despondently I picked up the volume for 1906-7, the years Evans had been in France, and chanced on the *Table des Gravures*, at the back of the volume, listing the 300 châteaux illustrated. In the course of an exciting half hour I found that of Evans's one hundred châteaux, sixty-one were illustrated in the *Annuaire*. Under each illustration was the name of the owner, and it would have been a simple matter for Evans to look him up and find both a country and a Paris address, as well as the nearest railway station. The bicycle tour suddenly became a reality.

Here too was the answer to many of the blanks I had drawn. Certain châteaux had been mis-spelt: Laudifer was Landifer, Louray was Lonrai, Grangefort was Lagrangefort and D'Anully was Avrilly. Evans, I surmised, had obtained a copy of the *Annuaire* and written to all, or nearly all, of the owners of the châteaux illustrated. Some probably did not reply, some may have refused, some château he may never have reached.

Evans is known to have taken infinite pains over his photographs. The story is told by George Bernard Shaw of his visit to Ely Cathedral, where for a fortnight he never set up his camera but simply studied the light. Then, one Saturday, he decided the light was right, and insisted that the nave be cleared of the chairs that had been neatly set out for Sunday's services. When the verger refused, Evans went over his head to the Dean. He also got a gas fitter to take down various lights that offended him.

As far as the châteaux were concerned, it is evident that Evans sometimes had both ample time and the freedom of the house. At Vaux-le Vicomte, for example, there is a photograph of a table laid for one; it is nice to think perhaps for Evans himself. In such cases Evans was able to wait, if necessary, for good weather, and catch exteriors with the light just clipping along a façade. Alex Starkey, however, points out that at other times Evans was not working in perfect conditions: at Boursault, for example, half the shutters are closed. This could hardly be artfulness on the part of Evans, because in another shot someone has opened a pair of shutters in a tower; there is also an iron bench turned across the front door.

Evans, one suspects, was sometimes there on sufferance with a house-keeper or gardener standing impatiently over him, he in turn feeling it impolitic to ask for furniture to be moved, even slightly. In one or two cases he catches the backs of chairs, which would have been out of the photograph if shifted just a few inches. The man who cleared the nave of Ely Cathedral would have avoided awkwardnesses such as these, and it is clear that some of Evans's photographs were taken on the hoof – as record shots – perhaps with a view to showing *Country Life* the château was worth a return visit. It is also inevitable that at some châteaux he would have encountered problems with building work. At Fontaine-Henry, in Normandy, there is a rare note by Evans: "must be revisited, château was largely under scaffolding for restoration". This might also explain, for example, why he did not take the classic view of Chenonceau across the water.

Perhaps the best portrait of Evans is provided by George Bernard Shaw, who was one of his most passionate admirers as well as one of the most enthusiastic and trenchant critics of the new art of photography:

"I cannot say exactly where I first met Evans. He broke in upon me from several directions simultaneously; and some time passed before I coordinated all the avatars into one and the same man. He was in many respects an oddity. He imposed on me as a man of fragile health, to whom an exciting performance of a Beethoven Symphony was as disastrous as a railway collision to an ordinary Philistine, until I discovered that his condition never prevented him from doing anything he really wanted to do, and that the things he wanted to do and did would have worn out a navvy in three weeks. Again he imposed on me as a poor man, struggling in a modest lodging to make a scanty income in a brutal commercial civilisation for which his organisation was far too delicate. But a personal examination of the modest lodging revealed the fact that this Franciscan devotee of poverty never seemed to deny himself anything he really cared for. It is true that he had neither a yacht, nor a couple of Panhard cars, not a liveried domestic staff, nor even, as far as I could ascertain, a Sunday hat. But you could spend a couple of hours easily in the modest lodging looking at treasures, and then stop only from exhaustion."

Shaw rated Evans as one of the two finest photographers of his age, and his high assessment was echoed by Alfred Stieglitz in America, who in 1903 hailed Evans as "the greatest exponent of architectural photography". Beaumont Newhall, a leading photographic historian, explains, in his excellent monograph on Evans, the impression made by an exhibition of the photographer's work which had been organised by the Royal Photographic

Creully

Ussé

De Tilly

Society of Great Britain in 1944, the year after Evans's death: "I wrote to my wife Nancy: 'Evans must be reckoned as one of the great pictorial photographers...his architectural photographs are the greatest of their kind, because he was able to combine a precision of definition with a softness and delicacy of gradation and because he had an extraordinary sense of scale and of light'."

Shaw, in his *Appreciation of Evans*, quoted above, touched on another key point: "Mr Evans made himself the most artistic of photographers by being the most simply photographic of artists." At this time, many photographers were seeking to emulate painting, and used every kind of soft-focusing to achieve painterly effects. While the results were certainly technically impressive, they also stand out with hindsight as being extraordinarily derivative. Evans, however, manifested an artistic eye in a very different way, and this emerges in his photographs of French châteaux as forcefully as his more famous photographs of cathedrals.

What stands out most strongly is Evans's sheer passion for architecture. His overriding desire was to communicate the power and the beauty of fine buildings. The châteaux fill his pictures; he rarely stood back and framed them with trees or a garden or parkland setting. Instead he used whatever lens or viewpoint would take him closest, not minding if the tops of chimneys, dormers or towers disappeared out of the top of the picture. Basically, Evans wanted his exteriors to overwhelm the viewer.

In some respects, Evans was like a modern day art editor, who 'crops' into a picture (often to the horror of the photographer) to make the image stronger. The difference is that Evans did his 'cropping' on the negative itself, deciding

De Tilly

the exact bounds of the picture himself. He liked his pictures to be printed and reproduced to the same dimensions as the negative, and this was a luxury which the large, early format of *Country Life* often allowed.

Evans was also a great exponent of the diagonal viewpoint. He rarely photographed a building head on. Even when confronted with a symmetrical classical façade, with a strong central axis running across the garden or courd d'honneur to the main entrance, Evans would almost invariably stand to the side. In this respect he was the opposite of today's designers, who like the graphic strength of an absolutely flat picture plane, and who prefer views of rooms which portray a single wall or are taken pointing into a corner showing two equal sides. Evans used diagonals in his photographs as powerfully and insistently as a Roman Baroque painter. He used them to create drama, to create a sense of space and depth, or conversely he used foreshortening so that a façade towers in front of the viewer. (The classic example is his view of the Ducal Palace at Nantes.)

There is also a parallel to be drawn between Evans's use of light and shade and the *chiaroscuro* of baroque painters. Evans was not imitating baroque painting, not perhaps even aware of it; he simply used compositional techniques that are similar and equally dramatic. With his interiors Evans had to rely on natural light. This was before the age of flash or floodlights, and many of the rooms – indeed houses – he photographed in had no electricity. Photographers did on occasion use magnesium powder, but this was both dangerous and produced clouds of smoke, and it is highly unlikely that Evans experimented with it in France. Instead he used the natural light of windows,

Avrilly

La Gascherie

often illuminating a picture by photographing from one space into another lighter space beyond – through a door onto a stair, or leaving a door open into a room beyond where sunlight was streaming in. When ceilings in dark rooms are particularly well lit it is possible that Evans used the technique adopted by later *Country Life* photographers: of angling mirrors inside or outside so they reflected light upwards. (Alternatively, he might have used sheets of white paper to the same end.)

Evans's exteriors have the strength and limitations of the orthochromatic film he used. This early type of film leaves skies a blank white or, at best, picks up only a hint of the fluffy clouds which modern panchromatic film catches to such good effect. Similarly, trees and shrubs appear as dense dark masses, adding drama, but giving the lasting impression that colourful, even gaudy, gardens of the early 1900s were immensely dark.

Evans was working at a time when *Country Life* photographers were their own masters, and the text accompanying his pictures rarely said much, or sometimes anything, about the architecture of the house, its furniture or gardens. Evans showed a remarkably sure eye, highlighting the finest and richest details as well as the most important features. But because he tended to home in on part of a façade, it can take the viewer a little time to work out how the different façades relate to each other – though he often provides just enough clues to fit the various shots together into a composite three-dimensional picture. However, the later *Country Life* tradition of standing back and showing the building descriptively and in full from each elevation of any note was completely alien to him. His concern was to convey character and atmosphere. "Try for a record of emotion rather than a piece of topography", he advised the beginner in a 1904 article in *American Photography*. "Wait 'till the building makes you feel intensely...then see what your camera can do towards reproducing that effect, that subject."

When I began hunting for Evans's châteaux it seemed inevitable that some of them would have been demolished or suffered through unsympathetic conversion to institutional use. In Britain, the toll of major country houses demolished in this century, mainly between 1920 and 1970, continues to mount. Of the English country houses illustrated in *Country Life* in the early 1900s, when it had the choice of all the houses in Britain, a painful number have gone. Many of the châteaux photographed by Evans could have been the subject of precisely the same criticisms made of ancestral houses in Britain: namely, that they were too large, too cold, too damp, too inconvenient. Yet of Evans's random selection of a hundred châteaux virtually every single one remains. The single loss is the Château de Moreuil, near Amiens, a casualty of the fierce fighting in the Somme during the 1914-18 war. A large number still belong to the descendants of the families which owned them in 1900. Many retain their contents, and an impressive number are open to the public. This provides an important antidote to the impression that French châteaux are all empty monuments like some of the most famous Royal Châteaux on the Loire. In Britain, the strongest tie in the middle years of this century was with the land, and if there was a choice the house went rather than the estate. In France, however, 'le château' represents something much more important:

15

ANTERROCHES

The snow-clad mountains in the background of Evans's photographs provide the clue that Anterroches is in the Massif Central. (Evans did not venture as far as the Pyrennees or the Alps.) The Anterroches are an ancient family known in the Auvergne since 1478, when Jean d'Anterroches bought the seigneurie from which he and his descendants have taken their name. Anterroches has the smooth, tall round towers that are typical of the Auvergne, with the local stone set in distinctive rough courses and little in the way of architectural features (*below*). Other examples include Anjony and Chevenon.

Characteristically Evans took the main front on the slant, his principal view (*overleaf*) including just enough of the angle tower to show you are looking at the corner of the building. His sure eye for important detail is shown in the photograph of the low wing attached to the château (*left*). This is clearly untouched by the restorer and has a typical, tall, Gothic ogee-headed door with roll mouldings – a fine example of the way Evans's photographs show the position of every stone (almost as precisely as modern photogrammetry) as well as the tooling or texture left on the surface by the mason.

The château stands just to the west of Murat, in Le Parc
Regional des Volcans d'Auvergne. It is listed as the seat of the
vicomte and vicomtesse d'Anterroches in the 1906-7 *Annuaire
des Châteaux*. The donjon itself dates from the 15th century, but
has been much remodelled and extended.

Louis XIV once referred to the castles of the Auvergne as
"nests for birds of prey". In contrast to the grand, often palatial
houses of Normandy and Burgundy, those of the Auvergne are of
a more rugged breed, with much more in common, spiritually,
with the tower houses of the Scottish border country.

The Auvergne Duchy was not finally united with France
until 1532, and defensibility continued to be a major considera-
tion until well into the 17th century. Rare is the château without a gun loop on either side of the front door: everywhere the
feeling is that the owners were like Patrick Forbes who, after the
sack of Corse Castle, Aberdeenshire, in 1550, resolved to build
"such a house as thieves will need to knock at ere they enter".

During the Hundred Years War much of the region suffered
at the hands of the free companies which occupied many of the
Auvergne fortresses. Later depredations came during the religious wars, and in the 17th century some of the most important
fortresses were deliberately slighted by Richlieu.

CHAPTER TWO

LA BASTIE D'URFÉ

When Evans arrived at La Bastie D'Urfé, it had been steadily falling into ruin for nearly a century. Three years later it was acquired by 'Diana', the strikingly named Historical Society of Forez. His photographs brilliantly capture the evocative beauty of the château, more Italian in spirit than any of the famous Renaissance châteaux of the Loire.

La Bastie d'Urfé was originally built for Claude d'Urfé (1501-58). Claude was a humanist, who later represented France at the Council of Trent and served as Ambassador in Rome. His grandson, Honoré d'Urfé wrote the famous romance *L'Astrée*.

Evans shows the house before later and largely sympathetic restoration. The first-floor windows then had 18th-century casements and louvre shutters, later replaced with stone mullions to match those above. The narrow 'Roman' style bricks of which the house is built are visible beneath the peeling stone.

Inside, the marvel of the house is the grotto, or 'Salle de Fraicheur' (*below*), which evidently appealed strongly to Evans as he took great trouble to record it in detail. The rough floor shown in his photographs has now been restored as a smooth and

intricate mosaic, but for the rest, Evans's photographs are proof of just how much is original in the elaborate encrustation of walls and ceiling (*above right*).

Theodore Cook, writing about the house in *Country Life*, in 1916, called for "a modern millionaire, like him who gave Langeais to the state, to recover and reunite the many treasures it has lost". There is, however, a small band of historic houses which are more atmospheric precisely because they are not lived in, and La Bastie d'Urfé remains one of them. Cook lamented the loss of the Sphinx that stood at the bottom of the ramp to the Louvre (*opposite and page 20*). A version of it has now been returned, and the rough twisted wire shown in the old windows of the grotto (*above left*) is now filled with trailing vines.

The marvel of the grotto was rather lost on Cook: "It's walls are covered in a curious dull mosaic of small pebbles, forming a yellowish background on which various designs are picked out in blue-grey, in white, or red, many of them in very high relief". But what pained him was the loss of contents.

BLOIS

Evans triumphantly captures the new monumentality that Francois I brought to French architecture at Blois, above all in the astonishing octagonal stair in the courtyard (*left*). But the remarkable part of his extensive coverage – over fifty negatives – is that he paid equal attention to almost every period of its architectural development: from Gothic and Renaissance, to the 17th-century Orléans wing by François Mansart, and the rich polychrome Victorian interiors.

From the early 13th century there is the cavernous Salle des Etats Généraux; Louis XII's filigree Gothic south wing (*page 31*) dates from 1498-1501. Evans took a beautiful photograph (*below*) looking through the inner arcade to the octagonal staircase, showing classical capitals set above columns and bases that are still Gothic.

Overlooking the town (*main picture overleaf*) François Premier built out a vast substructure to support a series of open loggias. (The arches are irregular because the medieval towers immediately behind had to be incorporated.)

When Gaston d'Orléans was exiled here because of his controversial intrigues at Court, he commissioned the young François

Mansart to design a vast new quadrangular palace that would have involved sweeping away all the earlier buildings. Only one range was executed, leaving two masterpieces strikingly juxtaposed. The interiors of the François I wing were extensively redecorated in 1845-48 by Félix Duban, Evans capturing his polychrome ceiling and wall paintings in pristine condition (*above, top, and page 30 top left*).

At Blois, Evans shows his penchant in photographing one space from another. For example, he squatted under the lower arches of the octagonal stair to show how the exquisite carving continued on the inner reveal (*page 29, top*), and he looked out at a staircase tower from an upstairs window (*page 29, bottom left*), catching the light on the leaded window pane as beautifully as a Dutch old master.

His photograph of the interior of the great octagonal stair (*page 28*) seems purposely taken to illustrate a point made in Theodore Cook's *The Spiral in Art* (1903). Cook was convinced that Renaissance architects had looked at spiral shells, and he used cutaway drawings to suggest that the twisting, plunging handrail at Blois was based on a study of the interior structure of the common form of shell: *Voluta vespertilio*. A special beauty

of the stair is the unusual serpentine shape of the steps (which Cook also insisted was taken from shells). Evans used light and shadow to perfection in highlighting this.

In a later book on the same theme, *The Curves of Life* (1914), Cook elaborated his theories of spirals still further, using several of Evans's photographs of the staircase at Blois to highlight his point: he believed it was not merely by an architect and master of construction, but a man who was a "decorative artist too", pointing to the sculptural treatment of the shells, the twisted capitals of the columns being carved at the sharpest angles.

Such curves, he argued, "can only have been designed by one who had carefully studied the forms of leaves and the arrangement of leaves upon a central stalk; by one who knew that Nature had no straight lines, and nearly all natural curves exhibit just this delicate mingling of the convex with the concave". All this led Cook to pronounce one name: Leonardo, who of course was living nearby at Amboise.

Though later historians rejected such attributions for lack of documentary evidence, Cook's theories take on renewed interest now that Leonardo's name is linked by modern scholars with Chambord. And whether Cook was correct or not in insisting

that French masons – and maybe Leonardo – were inspired by shells, his investigations of spiral forms anticipated by nearly a century the interest of modern architects in the subject.

Evans's sure eye for architecture is evident in his choice of details. For example, he photographed (*right and above right*) the ribs on the underside of the staircase and the delightful, late Gothic columns of the Louis XII wing carved with fleurs-de-lys.

The restoration had earlier won the approval of Theodore Cook, who wrote most of the *Country Life* articles that accompanied Evan's French photographs. In his *Memoirs of old Touraine*, Cook recalls that Balzac had been afraid later generations would know nothing of the château of Blois, save from his pages – so advanced in his day was the ruin and decay of the whole fabric. Cook thought the restoration "a lavishness of display, an ingenuity of detail, very rarely equalled", though he added "there is but little left to fancy in a restoration so painfully complete".

Comparing the excesses of restoration and decay, he concluded: "Blois is perhaps nearer to perfection than is Chinon, deserted, ruined, past recall. To few houses is it given, as to Langeais or Azay-le-Rideau, to escape decay and yet preserve the mellow beauty of the past."

CHAPTER FOUR

BOURSAULT

Evans's eye for the dramatic was rarely more apparent than in the photograph he took of this château soaring above the fir trees (*opposite*). The park plunges down to meet the drive, which rises steeply up to the house, and although the façade is barely glimpsed Evans has managed to capture in full the fairy-tale romance of Boursault's spiky silhouette.

Boursault was built by the celebrated Veuve Cliquot (née Ponsardin). She had bought the property – on the south bank of the River Marne – after the marriage of her daughter Clementine to the comte de Chevigné in 1817. Here a small château stood among the vines. Two decades later, when their daughter Marie-Clementine de Chevigné married the comte de Mortemart, Veuve Cliquot decided to build a new château taking advantage of the majestic panorama over the valley.

Arveuf, her architect, had worked on the restoration of Rheims Cathedral between 1842 and 1848. He erected a strictly symmetrical château in Renaissance style, with the elaborate ornament reaching a climax in the roof (*page 34, top and bottom right*). The dormers, with twin arches, are more elaborate than the windows of the main rooms below.

Perilously tall, thin chimneys vie in height with the candle-snuffer towers. The ridge of the roof has a cresting more elaborate than any balcony front. The Veuve Cliquot had the words 'Natis mater' – a mother to her children – inscribed on the façade.

The architect transformed the hillside into a vast landscape park in the English style, Evans capturing the spreading bows of the cedar trees and the walk winding into the woods (*page 33*). Here were belvederes and a basin of water with a 25 metre-high jet. A long straight allée led to a rocky outcrop and beyond to the woods on the plateau. Orchids grew in a hot house kept at 30° centigrade.

The château was sold in 1912, and sacked in 1945 following occupation by allied troops during the liberation of France. Today it belongs to M. Nourhan Fringhian.

Evans's photographs thus provide an important record of the house when it was furnished and still in its prime. Features of note include the chimneypieces (*right*) and boiseries in the saloon and dining room, which were carved by Clagman, and the the ceiling of the boudoir, which was painted by Levastre.

LA BRÈDE

La Brède is a French counterpart of Leeds Castle in Kent, set magically on two islands in the midst of a moat the size of a small lake *(opposite and below; page 39. above and top; and pages 40-1)*. And the English connections are manifold: The seigneurs of La Lande, who first built here, were allies of the kings of England to the end of the Hundred Year War. In the 18th century La Brède was the home of Montesquieu, the great writer, whose admiration for England led him to lay out a parc à l'anglaise in the style of William Kent. "We are planting woods and creating prairies", Montesquieu wrote to the Abbé Guasco. "Bring yourself to La Brede where you will find me in a true Gothic château, with charming environs for which I found inspirations in England."

In its essentials the château was given its present form in about 1420 by Jacques de La Lande. It is approached across two drawbridges leading from island to island. The first island is not so much an outer or stable court as a barbican or defence gateway. On the second island the buildings rise sheer from the water and are dominated by a round tower and a rectangular

donjon. During the 17th and 18th centuries it was remodelled to provide a greater degree of comfort, and part of the polygonal enceinte wall was demolished to provide a view across the courtyard from the moat.

Montesquieu was born at La Brède on January 18, 1689. In 1726 he abandoned a career of public service to make a series of travels to Italy, Germany, Holland and above all to England, where he spent two years. On his return he adopted the way of life of an English gentleman, living in the country and going to Paris but once a year. "What I love about La Brède is the feeling that my money is beneath my feet."

La Brède is south-west of Bordeaux, approached along the Roman road to Agen, which eventually leads to Toulouse. Ten miles from the city the road passes through the hamlet of La Prade. Two miles further on is the village of La Brède with its romanesque church – the château is a mile beyond.

Montesquieu's land included excellent vineyards. He produced a good white Graves, but his best wine was a red Graves from Rochemorin, which lies between Martillac and Léognan. This was highly prized, until the vineyard fell into decay during the 20th century. An active landlord, Montesquieu was vigorous

in maintaining his feudal rights as well as meeting his obligations to tenants. He was constantly buying and exchanging land: the archives of La Brède list forty-one purchases, twenty exchanges and six sales. It was also at La Brède that Montesquieu wrote *L'Esprit des Lois* and *Considerations on the causes of the Grandeur of the Romans and their decadence*.

La Brède became a shrine, though it did not appeal to every visitor. Stendhal in his *Voyage dans le Midi* described his visit thus: "Its the saddest country in the world. I saw a building without a façade, almost circular, surrounded by large moats, filled with water that was clean enough but the colour of coffee ...it reminded me of the château where Armide held the prisoners he had taken in the crusades."

Evans caught to perfection the way the château floats almost like a waterlily in a still flat landscape, showing the approach across the islands, and the little cottage-like, timber-framed structure perched over the entrance arch. His most atmospheric shot is of Montesquieu's bedroom (*pages 38-9, main picture*). With its dark panelling, double-banked portraits tilted at the top, it recalls the interiors of houses such as Knole in England.

Today La Brède is the property of the comtesse de Chabannes and the setting each year for a series of concerts.

CHAMBORD

Evans loved the sheer power of architecture. He rarely retreated far enough to show a whole building standing free in the landscape. His tendency was to 'crop in', like a modern art editor, to make the subject as dramatic and overwhelming as possible. While many architectural photographers would strain to include the tops of chimneys or cupolas, Evans happily cut them off (*page 45, bottom right*) in the interest of bringing the building closer to the viewer. For all the French love of symmetry and a strong central axis, Evans tended always to stand at one side.

His photograph of the courtyard (*opposite*) uses shadow in the arches to bring out the depth of modelling in the architecture; that of the main front (*below*) brilliantly captures the fairytale Gothic richness of the silhouette (*page 44,* detail). For though Chambord is often referred to as a hunting lodge, it is as much an expression of French ideals of kingship as Versailles. And kings, in demonstrating their lineage, invariably look backwards as well as forwards. So Chambord, with its huge round towers, has echoes of a medieval *donjon* or keep, while the celestial city on its roof draws inspiration from illuminated

manuscripts such as *Les Très Riches Heures du duc de Berry*.

François I ascended the throne in 1515 and building work was underway by 1519. It continued until his death in 1547, with a short break after his capture in Italy at the Battle of Pavia. The latest research convincingly suggests that Leonardo da Vinci, then living nearby at Amboise, had a strong hand in the design.

The three low wings of offices in front of the château were added by J.H. Mansart in the 1680s for Louis XIV, who came regularly to Chambord to hunt. Between 1725 and 1733, Stanislas Leczinski, the exiled King of Poland, lived at Chambord, and later marshal Saxe. The furniture largely disappeared during the Revolution, but in 1806 Napoleon granted Chambord to marshal Berthier.

Chambord and its park were classified as Monuments Historiques in 1840, just over a century before the first listing of inhabited buildings in England, and extensive repairs were carried out by the architects Desbois, father and son, for the comte de Chambord and his Bourbon-Parme nephews. Chambord was acquired by the State in 1930 and major works of repair, decoration and furnishing are now underway.

CHAPTER SEVEN

CHANTILLY

Evans's photography of Chantilly, perhaps more than any other château, demonstrates that he was in a class of his own. For Chantilly was photographed by numerous photographers (great and unknown), and illustrated in an excellent exhibition catalogue: *Le Domaine de cantilly vu par les photographes du XIXe siècle* (1993).

Chantilly is a vast spreading composition seen isolated in an even vaster park, and the temptation is to stand back and use a wide lens to capture its breathtaking extent. Evans, however, did the opposite, moving in close to capture the sheer monumentality of the building better than anyone before or since. His views brilliantly reveal its robustness by allowing you all the time to look into it and through it (as *left*). His views of the great outdoor staircase (*below*) and the open arcades in the courtyard (*page 48, middle left*), all taken at an angle, have the quality of 18th-century stage sets by the Bibiena family – with backcloths showing palaces composed of endless arcades and open courtyards.

Chantilly, for all its illustrious history was, when Evans saw it, little more than 10 years old. The grand château of the prince

de Condé had been razed to the ground at the Revolution, the furniture sold, and the estate parcelled off. When the last Condé died mysteriously in 1830 he left his estates (returned to him at the Restoration) to Henri d'Orléans, duc d'Aumale, one of the sons of Louis-Philippe. The duc was one of France's greatest collectors and connoisseurs, and between 1875 and 1882 he rebuilt the grand château on its original foundations, his architect, Daumet, freely interpreting the original design and using the unusual triangular layout to dramatic effect.

In addition to some of the majestic interiors (such as *bottom left and overleaf*), Evans's best photographs are of the magnificent marble staircase. For once he chose an exactly axial viewpoint, perhaps because the swirling curves of the rich scrolled balustrades provided all the movement and drama he felt he needed.

The first château at Chantilly, dating from the 10th century, had been destroyed in 1358. In 1486 Pierre d'Orgemont, chancellor of France, constructed a second fortress on the same site in the middle of a lake on a triangular plan which has always been respected in later remodellings. In 1450, Marguerite, the heiress of the Orgemonts, married the baron de Montmorency.

Guillaume de Montmorency reconstructed the chapel in 1522. To his eldest son, Anne, he gave both Chantilly and Ecouen. At Chantilly, Anne employed Pierre Chambiges I, the mason responsible for the transept of Senlis Cathedral, to work on the interior courtyard. In 1538 he added a large raised terrace. Then in 1550-60 he employed the architect Jean Bullant, who worked for him at Ecouen, to build the petit château on a separate island – the one element of the Renaissance work that has survived.

After Anne de Montmorency was killed in 1567 fighting the Protestants, a new chapter opened when the Grand Condé, so named because of his prowess on the battlefield, employed Le Nôtre and La Quintinie to design vast gardens (details *above and left*), and construct the spectacular outdoor staircase, le Grand Degré, photographed so dramatically by Evans.

Towards the end of his life Condé commissioned Jules Hardouin-Mansart, the architect of Versailles, to rebuild the château, with less happy results. Between 1719 and 1735 the architect Jean Aubert built the stupendous Grandes Ecuries. In 1772 Louis Joseph de Bourbon, prince de Condé (1736-1818) created an English park, complete with a rustic hameau, which survives to this day.

CHAPTER EIGHT

CHASTELLUX

Evans captured the spirit of this plain but imposing château with its massive towers rising above bastion walls (*opposite and pages 54 and 55*). The oldest parts of the building date back to the 12th century, the huge circular towers to the 15th.

Among the more notable proprietors have been Artaud de Chastellux, who travelled to Vézelay in 1146 to hear Saint Bernard preaching the crusade in which he took part with his five sons. Later, Claude de Beauvoir, sire de Chastellux (1386-1453) became chamberlain to Jean the Fearless, marshal of France, and captain general of Normandy. His seizure of Cravant in 1423 won him and his descendants the position of hereditary first canon of the Cathedral of Auxerre.

During the 18th century, François-Jean, marquis de Chastellux, who was a soldier and writer of talent, distinguished himself in the Seven Years War and the War of American Independence, and published in 1764 an interesting tome: *Voyage dans l'Amérique septentrionale*. Henri-Georges-César de Chastellux, who fled France in 1791 following the Revolution, was able to reclaim his château in 1810. His son, Henri-Louis, was created duc de Rauzan-Duras in 1819, on his marriage to the only

daughter of the duc de Duras, while his brother, César-Laurent, inherited the château, which was now on the point of ruin: "When I became proprietor of the château of Chastellux after 1816 I took a vow to make it habitable and by the work of restoration to establish myself and my successors in the country in which my family had lived for so many centuries." César-Laurent had only daughters, one of whom married her cousin Amédée de Chastellux, and the château has remained in the family ever since.

Despite evident remodelling and restoration, the treatment fell far short of what a Viollet-le-Duc would have done. The château maintains many irregularities which speak of change over the centuries: towers of varying sizes, 18th-century casement windows, and early 19th-century pointed arches coupled with a pretty horseshoe stair in troubadour style. When Evans came the leaves were barely on the trees but he took an evocative shot of a wooden bridge leading across to the gardens (*page 53*).

CHAPTER NINE

CHÂTEAUDUN

Evans caught the haunting presence of this imposing château, long left to slow decay and, even then, an ancient monument more than an ancestral family seat. It towers over the quiet waters of the Loir, built out on massive retaining walls, in much the same way as Warwick Castle looms above the River Avon. Evans, uncannily emphasises its sheer height by photographing it at a moment when the roofs almost disappear into the mist (*opposite*).

The name Châteaudun holds memories of a Celtic rather than a Roman oppidum, giving title in turn to the feudal lords of the place, the comtes de Dunois. From the 12th century survives the imposing circular donjon or keep. Its twin round-headed windows are still Norman. Inside are three sets of lodgings, one above the other, two with impressive vaults.

"Le jeune et beau Donois", of a famous song, was a companion in arms of Joan of Arc from the first, defending Orleans against Talbot and going on with her to liberate Chartres, Saint-Denis and Paris itself. It was he who transformed the fortress into a grand seigneurial residence. He began by reconstructing the chapel next to the Romanesque donjon. Inside, the chapel

unusually, has two levels: the lower, or seigneurial chapel, which is vaulted, and the upper chapel for the household, with its wooden roof en carène looking like an upturned boat.

The west wing was begun in 1460, with a spiral stair in a projecting tower. When Dunois died in 1468 this was completed by his son, François de Longueville, who also began the staircase in the north wing. This was, in turn, completed from 1511, by his son François II, 1st duc de Longueville.

The magnificant scale of Châteaudun is evident in the courtyard. The Longueville wing consists of two tall storeys of even height with two spectacular staircases. These are not built as projecting towers, but integrated into the corps-de-logis. Outside, the main staircase is still Gothic – a virtuoso display of filigree carving. The four tiers of flattened arches, gradually diminishing in height towards the top, are flanked by butresses that are hardly recognisable beneath such a wealth of spiral colonettes, corbels, ogee arches, niches and hoods. Added depth is given by the outer arches, which are carved with rich trefoils and pendants.

The treatment becomes more sober towards the top, with the plainest of pyramid roofs flanked by cylindrical tourelles where

the carved detail is restricted to the windows. Within the arches the details suddenly become classical – stone balustrades and cornices which in character belong to a different building.

In the north wing are to be found some Renaissance details of great beauty. Here Evans took one of his most evocative photographs (*opposite*) – standing on the spiral stair (just catching the plunging hand rail) and showing the Renaissance doorhead juxtaposed with the rich gothic carving outside. The frieze over the door, which caught Evans's eye, is carved in low relief and is of remarkable crispness and clarity – the capitals being more like corbels. Another photograph shows the covered wall-walk (*page 37*) complete with holes in the floor for dropping missiles or boiling oil on attackers.

In 1710 Châteaudun passed by marriage to Charles Philippe d'Albert, duc de Luynes and de Chevreuse. In 1723 the town was almost completely destroyed in a fire and the Duc opened the château to the townspeople. Unfortunately, interiors were crudely altered, and the château entered a long period of decline, suffering badly at the Revolution. However, in the 1930s the state bought it, and it has now been scrupulously repaired by the Monuments Historiques.

CHAPTER TEN

CHÂTEAU-
GAILLARD

"How beautiful is my year-old daughter", exclaimed Richard Cœur de Lion, on seeing his new castle. He had every reason to be proud. Château-Gaillard was not only one of the great masterpieces of western medieval military architecture, it was also completed with astonishing speed between 1196 and 1197-

Richard I became King of England and Duke of Normandy in 1189, but had been taken prisoner in Germany on his return from the third Crusade, where he remained incarcerated until, as legend recalls, his faithful minstrel found him. Freed in 1194, Richard was forced to accept, by the terms of the Treaty of Issoudun, the loss of the great fortress of Gisors, built by William Rufus to defend the frontier of Normandy with France. Château-Gaillard, standing high on a spur above the Seine,

was built to make good this loss. A small triangular fort, flanked by towers, protected the most vulnerable flank. This front was separated from the castle proper by a deep ditch cut in the chalk – the two being linked by a drawbridge.

Both the triangular fort and the outer enceinte of the main castle had largely vanished by the time Evans arrived. What stands out in his photographs is the central keep surrounded by an elliptical mantle wall (*left and page 60*). This is in the form of a continuous series of half towers, curiously like a giant jelly mould, designed to eliminate any blind angles of fire. Towering above them, the walls of the keep were steeply battered, so that projectiles striking them would simply ricochet. However, this impregnable fortress was taken in less than 10 years. After Richard's death in 1199, his great rival Philip Augustus of France claimed Normandy and laid seige. Five months later the French made a surprise entry through the castle's latrines. Though fighting continued for another month, the English garrison never succeeded in withdrawing to the keep.

In 1315 the unfortunate Queen Marguerite of Burgundy was imprisoned in the castle, and strangled here on the orders of her husband, the future Louis X. The castles defences were put to the test again after the battle of Agincourt. Château-Gaillard was the last stronghold (apart from Mont St Michel) to hold out against Henry V, succumbing four years later in 1419.

Recovered in 1449 by Charles VII, the castle was used by members of the League resisting Royal troops in 1596, and was dismantled in 1603 by Henri IV, and subsequently by Richelieu.

Evans set out to capture the heroic beauty of the site, showing to spectacular effect how it not only dominated the Seine but commanded the whole landscape around (*above and page 63, top right*). One of his most evocative photographs portrays the castle looming above a sunlit street in Le Petit Andely (*left*), which happily escaped the bombardment which largely destroyed Le Grand Andely, just up the road, in 1940.

Theodore Cook took the view that "it was the very complication of Richard's defensive works" which "prevented his garrison from using their full strength. The network of fortified posts had only served as an assistance to the besiegers who took them one after another with attacks by overwhelming numbers."

CHAPTER ELEVEN

CHAUMONT

Evans photographed Chaumont in its second age of splendour. In 1875 the estate had been purchased by an heiress, Marie-Charlotte-Constance Say, who that year married Prince Amédée de Broglie (1849-1917). He was the second son of Duke Albert de Broglie, Senator and President of the Council of State. They engaged the fashionable architect Paul-Ernest Sanson (1838-1918) to restore and modernise the castle, and lived at Chaumont like royalty, entertaining princes and maharajahs. Chaumont stands in a commanding position above the Loire, and from the 11th century belonged to the illustrious house of Amboise. Pierre d'Amboise (d.1473) began the reconstruction of the château on the present quadrangular plan. Completion was left to his grandson Charles II d'Amboise, who inherited in 1481 and also carried out a major remodelling of the Château de Meillant in Berry (see Chapter 24), in 1500-10. Charles II was grand maître de la Maison du roi, both marshal and admiral of France, and was made Governor of Milan by Louis XII. While he was in Italy it is thought he entrusted the building works to his uncle, the famous cardinal d'Amboise, first Minister to Louis XII, who had transformed

the Château de Gaillon in Renaissance style.

Evans photographed the entrance towers (*page 66*), which carry a carved band of interlaced 'C's for Charles d'Amboise and his emblem of burning rocks (chaud mont – *page 69, top left*). Over the entrance are the fleurs-de-lys of France and the monographs of Louis XII and Anne of Brittany. Characteristically, Evans came in close to emphasise the bulk of the towers; from further back the château appears to lie low in relation to the park, an effect Evans evidently wanted to avoid.

In 1560 Chaumont had been acquired by Catherine de Medici, with the intention of forcing Diane de Poitiers to exchange it for Chenonceau. In the early 19th century, Chaumont stood empty and decaying until acquired in the 1830s by the comte d'Aramon, who began repairs. After his death in 1847 his widow married the vicomte de Walsh, who entrusted the restoration to the architect Jules Potier de La Morandière. Evans arrived when the further restoration by Sanson was complete.

Evans's photographs show some of the main rooms furnished in a manner typical of that date, with chests, coffers and elaborately carved tables and tapestries lining the walls (*page 67*). One of the stone fireplaces is flanked with suits of armour and

emblazoned with a display of pikes and spears (*above*), while at the far end of the dining room is an immensely rich, carved Gothic fireplace (*top*) designed by Sanson.

One of Sanson's additions was the richly carved Flamboyant Gothic balcony (*left*) along the east side of the courtyard. Though no trace of this survived when he began work, Sanson was able to reconstruct it from a description by Félibien in 1681: "All along the first floor is a sort of hewn stone terrace some five or six feet wide. It is supported by rows of great shells placed one above the other, themselves supported by brackets decorated with masks and the coat-of-arms of the Amboise house and families by marriage."

Before Sanson arrived the rich octagonal staircase in the courtyard (a Gothic version of that at Blois) had been brutally truncated. Evans's photograph (*page 69, top left*) shows the exquisite scrolls of the classical acanthus carved on a shield surmounted by the Cardinal's hat, as well as the remarkable pattern of lead glazing which survived later alterations. Inside, the broad spiral stair (*page 68*) naturally attracted Evans's interest – its Gothic colonettes and ogee arches framing Renaissance shell-headed niches.

CHAPTER TWELVE

CHAUMONT LA GUICHE

The domain of Chaumont was acquired by Marie de Lespinasse, the wife of Jean de La Guiche, and their son Girard between 1406 and 1421. The present château was built by Pierre de La Guiche between 1500-1514. The main elements of this date to survive are the south-west range and the large cylindrical Amboise tower *(below and overleaf, bottom left)*

Pierre de La Guiche, whose wife was a niece of the great Jaques d'Amboise, arranged the marriage between Henri and Catherine de Medici, while his grandson Philibert was bailli de Macon, governor of the Lyonnais, and then grand master of the Royal Artillery. He refused to take part in the St Bartholomew's Day Massacre when thousands of Protestants were slaughtered. The remarkable stables were constructed by his eldest daughter Henrietta, to house the horses of her second

husband, Louis-Emmanuel de Valois, duc d'Angoulême and son of Charles de Valois, the bastard son of Charles IX.

In 1763 Jean de La Guiche became proprietor. He had married Mlle de Verneuil, daughter of the duc de Bourbon, first Minister of Louis XV. During the 1850s the château was remodelled in revival style, and it remains the property of the marquis de La Guiche.

Evans captured the full drama of the remarkable stables (*right*), the finest in France after those at Versailles and Chantilly. The design is highly unusual, dominated by giant outdoor staircases rising to the first floor in double ramps – you could almost say a horseshoe. As at certain quintas in the north of Portugal, the stairs are grander than the building behind.

Over the central entrance (*page 72*) is a lifesize equestrian statue of the owner, suitably emblazoned with military trophies such as canons and cannon balls. While the stonework of the walls is quite rough, the huge chimneys are faced with strongly blocked masonry and capped by segmental pediments that are, in appearance, almost like sarcophagi.

The stalls for the horses are arranged on either side of a columned nave supporting a beautiful cross-vaulted ceiling. The

architect was Francois Martel "dit" Champagne. The contract for the carpentry states a payment of "910 livres, deux bottes et une anné de vin, dix bichats de seigle, 100 livres de lard.

The 1850s work is a characteristic mix of late Gothic and Renaissance detail, such as extravagant dormers and rich cresting and finials, particularly on the square corner towers. Inside this is echoed by a beautiful Gothic-Revival stair (*above*) ascending in broad flights under a graceful pendant vault. The main salon (*page 74 top left*), hung with tapestries, also has a full-height Gothic fireplace of this date. Another salon (*left*) has 18th-century panelling.

W.H. Ward, who wrote the article on the château in *Country Life* on January 27, 1917, complained that it "seems to have suffered that drastic process of 'restoration' so dear to the hearts of the French owners and architects". Inside, he said, it was hard to judge "how far what we now see represents the original work and how far it is the product of an archaesing imagination...Of the furniture of the Dining-room and its unfinished chimney-pieces in the manner of the early 16th century, the less said the better".

CHAPTER THIRTEEN

CHEMAZÉ

Chemazé is a modest château, made remarkable by a superlative Renaissance tower (*below*). Evans must have been led here by an illustration in the *Annuaire des Châteaux*. Also known as the Château de St Ouen, it stands not 500 yards from the village of Chemazé, north-north-west of Angers, near Château-Gontier. It used to belong to a community of Augustins, who remained proprietors until the Revolution, and here, early in the 16th century, the abbot, Guy Le Clerc, decided to build himself a house worthy of his rank; he was chaplain successively to two Queens: Anne of Brittany and Claude of France.

To a 13th-century logis the abbot added a bravura tower (*page 81*) in the middle of the façade containing a spiral stair. The whole is a rich mix of Gothic and Renaissance motifs that characterise the Renaissance in the Loire. In this case there is more than a hint of Portuguese Manueline style in the clustered and spirally twisted columns at the corners and the domed bartizans at the top, which recall the contemporary tower of Belem outside Lisbon.

Evans's photograph of the entrance (*opposite*) captures the richness of invention: spirally twisted classical columns framing the

door with inner colonettes that are still Gothic, while the capitals of the columns are set diamond fashion by a mason who had evidently decided it was better to show two complete faces rather than one as is usual with an Ionic pilaster.

Above are more characteristic details: candelabra, cherubs, and a shell stretched out to the proportions of a fan. At the top, instead of battlements there is a miniature arcade with ornamental wheels inset in the parapet. All the windows are vertically linked, framed by a series of short and long pilasters that stand strangely one on top of another.

The name of Simon Hayeneuve has been put forward as architect, his works including the roodscreen at Le Mans Cathedral, the chasse of Sainte Scolastique du Mans, and the reliquary of Notre-Dame de L'Epine at Evron – all of which are in the vicinity.

Inside, Evans recorded a spectacular stone chimneypiece (*above*), presumably inspired by an engraving – again Gothic in form, but Renaissance in detail. The Gothic wing beside the tower (*right*) is modest, like a rectory.

CHAPTER FOURTEEN

CHEVERNY

The main front of Cheverny (*below*) is photographed – usually with huntsmen and hounds in the foreground – almost as much as Azay-le-Rideau and Chenonceau. Typically, Evans chose strongly diagonal viewpoints rather than the more usual frontal shot. A head-on view highlights Cheverny's one weakness as a composition: the narrow centrepiece is overwhelmed by the massive end pavilions. This is not apparent in Evans's diagonal views which emphasise the strength of modelling and liveliness of detail.

It is doubtful if a better picture has ever been taken of the rear front (*opposite*), which recalls Piranesi in the steepness and drama of its perspective. Here the diagonal view shows the advances and recessions of the façade as well as the deeply inset windows.

An early 16th-century château on the site was rebuilt in 1625-30 for Henri Hurault, Governor and bailiff of Blois. In contrast to the common practice of retaining corner towers to proclaim a sense of ancestry, all trace of the earlier château was

obliterated. The master mason who carried out the work was Jacques Bougier, who was also heavily involved in the contemporary rebuilding of the château of Blois.

Inside, Evans's interest was caught by the beautiful carved detail of the staircase (carved with the initials 'FL 1634') and the elaborate Louis XIII boiseries of the main rooms (*opposite*). Some of the original work is overlaid with rather good 19th-century remodelling and repainting. He was also drawn to the richly treated double-decker chimneypieces rising to the ceilings (*right*), and a beautiful chest (*above*). Much of the decorative paintings in these rooms is attributable to Jean Mosnier of Blois, and his atelier.

When Henri Hurault, comte de Cheverny, died in 1648, he left the estate to his daughter Cécile, marquise de Montglat. Subsequently the château passed through various hands before being bought back by Anne Denis Hurault, marquis de Vibraye, whose descendants own it today.

In the 19th century the parterres were replaced with jardins à l'anglaise, but the spectacular avenue, five miles in length, aligned on the entrance front, remains.

CHAPTER FIFTEEN
COURTANVAUX

Close to, Courtanvaux has the severity of a house in Scotland, without a trace of decorative carving and hardly a moulding (*opposite*). However, Evans walked round to the meadow below the house where it stands picturesquely on a high terrace, wonderfully enfolded in deep woods (*page 89, top*). Here is a chapel, a corbelled tower, and one of the delightful domed towers that frame the entrance.

Courtanvaux has passed by marriage through four families. The property was brought in 1465 by Jacques de Berziau, secretary of Charles VIII, who made him controller general of his Finances. He began the present house in the late 15th century. His daughter and heiress married Antoine de Souvré, a soldier who served Louis XII and François I with distinction. To him is due one of the charming entrance archways, flanked by a pair of circular domed towers with exuberant classical detail of the very early Renaissance (*below*). Evans took a close-up detail of the remarkable dormer windows on the towers (*page 89, bottom left*). Their monumentality is quite different from the usual pierced and filigree work of the late Gothic and

Renaissance dormers. Evans's lens highlights the playful use of classical details, notably pairs of taller pilasters framing a shorter one in the centre. A head-on symmetrical shot (*opposite*) focuses attention on the superb detail of the archway, notably the incised Greek key pattern. And Evans uses sunlight and shadow, as masterfully as a Roman baroque architect, to highlight the strength of modelling in the niches and pediments above.

In 1609, Courtanvaux was raised to a marquisate by Henri IV, in favour of Gilles de Souvré, Governor of the Dauphin – the future Louis XIII – who in turn made him a gentleman of the bedchamber and marshal of France in 1615. His great grand-daughter, Anne de Souvré, married Michel Le Tellier, Marquis de Louvois, the celebrated minister of Louis XIV. His descendants retained the domain until 1781, when Louise Le Tellier married the comte de Montesquiou-Fezansac, who became chamberlain to the Emperor.

In 1882, after the death of comte Odon de Montesquiou, his widow redecorated the interior in the historicizing taste of the period. For once, however, Evans did not gain entry to take photographs. Today, Courtanvaux is the property of the commune of Bessé-sur-Braye, and is open to the public.

CHAPTER SIXTEEN

ERMENONVILLE

Evans photographed few 18th-century châteaux, and characteristically his pictures here are all taken off-axis, and never show the whole château standing free across the park. Instead, there are glimpses of a tower and a wing standing in the moat (*page 93, top right and page 94, bottom right*), while in his photograph of the cour d'honneur (*overleaf*) Evans crops out the wings to give greater presence to the corps-de-logis and its richly sculptured pediment.

Ermenonville was rebuilt in the first half of the 18th century by the Lombard family. As was often the custom in France, they paid homage to the history of the place by retaining the quadrangular medieval plan, the moat and the circular corner towers. In 1754, the fermier général, René Hatte, acquired the property, and was succeeded in 1763 by his grandson René, marquis de Girardin. The marquis had travelled extensively in England and had been enraptured by the new naturalistic style of landscape gardening there. Employing gardeners from Scotland, he created, between 1766 and 1770, one of the very first examples of a jardin à l'anglaise in France – contemporary with the parc Monceau in Paris and, close to Ermenonville

itself, the gardens at Chantilly, Mortefontaine and Betz. Here was a landscape of lakes, islands, grottoes and cascades (*page 90; page 94, top; and page 95*), and one which evidently appealed to Evans for its picturesque qualities.

Girardin had visited England in 1763 and admired William Shenstone's ferme ornée at the Leasowes. While the naturalistic style in England dates back to the 1730s, when William Kent first "lept the fence and saw all nature was a garden", it was only after 1760 that the landscape style became dominant in England. In France, the more usual style of jardin anglais was a small, irregular area laid out beside the usual parterres. Girardin's estate, which amounted to some 900 hectares, was on the scale of the largest English parks.

The marquis de Girardin was a close friend of the philosopher Jean-Jacques Rousseau, who also inspired the move away from the traditional formal garden. Six months before Rousseau's death, the marquis persuaded him to retire to Ermenonville. The great man declined to stay in the château, retiring instead to the gate lodge. In an archpiece of Romanticism, Rousseau was entombed at midnight in a solemn torchlit ceremony on the island of poplars in the middle of the lake. On his sarcophagus, designed by the painter Hubert Robert, and sculpted by J.P. Lesueur, was inscribed: "Ici repose l'homme de la nature et de la verité." Rousseau's remains were

transferred in 1794 to the Pantheon, but the island, ringed by Lombardy poplars, remains as a poignant reminder.

The association was inevitably made between the naturalistic style and the English love of freedom. Rousseau's belief that man is by nature virtuous and happy, but is corrupted by society, appealed to Girardin.

The marquis explained his method of design in his 'Essay on Landscape': First you begin with a rough sketch. Then an assistant places rods in the ground to indicate contours, vistas and the outline of paths and plantations. Where water was proposed, a white cloth was spread on the ground to suggest the effect and help determine the outline. Thus from the château was a view carefully composed to evoke a Claude Lorraine landscape.

In 1938 the park around the château was acquired by the Touring Club de France.

CHAPTER SEVENTEEN

ESCLIMONT

In the 11th century the seignurie of Esclimont belonged to the family of Escrones, passing by marriage to the Blaru, Trie and d'Allonville families. The present château (*below and page* 99) was begun in 1543 by Étienne du Poncher, Archbishop of Tours. The grandson of Jean Poncher, goldsmith of Charles VIII and Louis XII, Étienne served as a member of the Grand Conseil. On his death, in 1552, the château passed to his sister and heir, Marguerite Poncher, and then to her brother-in-law Philippe Hurault, comte de Cheverny. In 1639 Henri Hurault, Governor of Chartres, sold Esclimont to the powerful Claude de Bullion, a conseiller d'État and surintendant des Finances.

For three further centuries it passed by inheritance. At the end of the reign of Louis XIV, Charles-Denis de Bullion, marquis de Gallardon, transformed the château in classical style, leaving little trace of medieval or Renaissance work though, as usual, retaining the circular towers at the corners. Inside fine Régence boiseries remain from this period. The last marquis, on his death in 1769, left the property to his niece the duchesse de Laval. She left it, in turn, to her daughter the duchesse

FRANÇOIS·DE·LA·ROCHEFOUCAULD

de Luynes. Her daughter, the duchesse Mathieu de Montmorency gave it to her grandson, the vicomte Sosthène de La Rochefoucauld, Duke first of Bisaccia, then of Doudeauville. In 1865 the duc de Doudeauville commissioned the architect Henri Parent to restore and remodel the château in a rich Renaissance style, entrusting the layout of the park – in English style – to the Buehler brothers.

In 1968 Esclimont was acquired from the Rochefoucaulds by M. René Traversac for his chain of châteaux-hotels. Today, the massive 14th-century gatehouse (*page 96 and detail above*), topped by a steep pyramid roof, has alone largely escaped later remodelling. It has the characteristic machicoulis supporting a covered wall walk.

Evans's photographs capture the decorative treatment of the dormers and bartisans, as well as the pierced cresting along the ridge of the roof. Characteristically, the dormer windows are more elaborate than those below, and are emphasised by striking chequerwork bands of alternating squares of stone and brick.

Once again Evans 'crops' into his subject, showing little foreground and cutting into finials, and even the cupola, in the interest of bringing the architecture forcefully before the viewer.

CHAPTER EIGHTEEN

CHÂTEAU D'EU

The château d'Eu has an illustrious history. Here William the Conqueror married Matilda of Flanders – an event portrayed in the Bayeux tapestry – though no trace of this château remains. And here, close to the sea, duc Henri de Guise in 1578 commissioned an architect from Beauvais, Claude Leroi, to build him a summer house. His widow, Catherine of Cleves, continued the work – intending to build two wings forming a U-shaped courtyard. Only one of these was constructed and vanished long ago. Following the murder of the duc de Guise at Blois in 1588, Catherine came frequently during her 45 years as a widow and built the chapel of the neighbouring Jesuit college and commissioned the magnificent Guise tombs.

In 1660, La Grande Mademoiselle, Louis XIV's cousin, acquired the estate, added wings and laid out extensive parterres. In 1821 the future King Louis-Philippe restored the château, and in 1843 and 1845 received Queen Victoria in lavish style. The château, inevitably, was confiscated with the Second Empire, but in 1874 restored at the request of Louis-Philippe's grandson, the comte de Paris. Repairs and redecoration were carried out under the great Viollet-le-Duc, who also restored

Pierrefonds. For Eu, he designed the furniture as well.

The escalier d'honneur was entirely remodelled by Viollet-le-Duc in 1675. To the north, the ground floor apartment (*page 100*) was decorated by the duchesse d'Orléans, daughter-in-law of Louis-Phillippe. From this period the marquetry floors remain. The painted walls and ceilings, together with the Brazilian and Portuguese furniture, were introductions of the comtesse de Paris

Following a fire in 1902, the château was again restored by the comte d'Eu, son-in-law of the Emperor of Brazil, and grandfather of the present comtesse de Paris. In 1962, the château was acquired by the département of Eu and reopened nine years later as the Louis Philippe Museum.

Evans's photographs record the formal planting of the parterres as well as a spectacularly overarched allée (*page 104*). He photographed the main fronts (*page 101*) at an angle to give modelling to the rather flat façades. Inside, he had to cope with the problems of dark interiors, at a time when flashlights and floodlighting had yet to be invented. In the dining room (*right*), where the corners in particular are dark, he managed to get a strikingly strong light on the ceiling. This may have been done with the help of mirrors – inside or outside the room – a practice of a later *Country Life* photographer A.E. Henson.

One of Evans's most atmospheric photographs shows a glazed corridor (*page 102, top left*) with banquettes and tables covered with carpets, and numerous trophies of antlers along the walls. He also photographed the Chambre de la Grande Mademoiselle (*above left*), where Viollet-le-Duc shows he could turn his hand to 17th-century boiseries as well as Gothic. Characteristically for the 17th century, the walls are divided into three tiers of panelling emblazoned with the interlaced monogram of the Grand Mademoiselle: AMLO, standing for Anne Marie Louise d'Orléans. Another room (*above right*) has a florid wallpaper suggestive of seahorses and a rich frieze of a type much used by Viollet-le-Duc.

CHAPTER NINETEEN

LA GRANGEFORT

This château, confusingly, is sometimes spelt as one word – Lagrangefort – and sometimes as two or three. It is situated in the heart of the Auvergne, in the hills south of Clermont Ferrand, just outside the village of Les Pradeaux, south of Issoire. With its battlements and slender corner towers, the château has a distinct toy-fort look. For all its machicoulis and crenellations it can never have been a serious defence, as is evident from the large windows, balconies, and even a clock set into the battlements. Other playful details are buttresses at the corners of the towers, rising no more than a single storey. What is puzzling is that the masonry varies strongly in character. One tower is in smooth ashlar, another in rougher, irregularly coursed stone. The impression is of a building spanning the centuries, part late medieval, part 19th-century-castle revival. Certain details are curiously exaggerated as they might be in a toy fort. The bartisans on either side on the clock tower have vastly enlarged arrow slits. The battlements above (*as opposite*) also have individual arrow slits, as if to allow archers to shoot through them as well as between them.

The most interesting aspect of Evans's photographs are the interiors. Here is a complete and typically cluttered 19th century arrangement. The vaulted ceilings may be old, but they have all been painted with borders and star patterns. The walls have gothic papers or stencils (*as left*). In one saloon the hooded chimneypiece (*left*) has been painted with portraits and a landscape, in others the elaborate fire-dogs and fire-backs can be seen (*page 111*). All the rooms are still lit by candles, with chandeliers, candlesticks and wall brackets at the ready. In the bedroom (*page 110, right*) an elaborate four-poster stands on a raised dais.

The outline of the château's history is given in the *Dictionnaire Historique de Tardieu*. The château was given the name of La Grangefort to distinguish it from nearby places called La Grange. The first seigneur was Jacques d'Ambilion in 1370. Morinot d'Ambilion, dean of the cathedral of Clermont, sold it in 1445 to Hugues de Pons, with whose descendants it was to remain for 400 years.

In 1592 Gilbert de Pons was charged to defend Nonette and Usson against the League, and saw his château burned and

pillaged as a result. The château was, however, rebuilt, and was only sold following the death of Antoine de Pons, bishop of Moulins, in 1849. His nephew, Antoine-Arthur, on inheriting, sold the château to M. le vicomte Marie-Victor de Matherel, chevalier of the Légion d'honneur and treasurer-general of Puy-de-Dome.

The Vicomte employed M. Vianne as architect to restore the château and provide it with feudal trappings: namely, a draw-bridge and Gothic balconies. The *Dictionary* describes as note-worthy "a vestibule adorned with knights' armour, and the arms of all the grand masters of the Order of St John, antique furni-ture, objects d'art, a magnificent salon, a superb gothic dining room, a library filled with rare and curious books and, with it all, the exceptional intelligence and affability of the châtelain".

Today, La Grangefort is a camping site boasting a large open-air swimming pool which sits right in front of the château. The proprietor is M. Van Bronkhorst.

Fourteen of Evans's negatives are in the *Country Life* archive. In addition the pictures already referred to, they include an old chair in the hall (*page 109, top right*), a family living room (*page 107*) and a dining room (*above*).

HAUTEFORT

The Château d'Hautefort has an unusual English connection: Dante consigned its 12th-century owner to hell for having set father against son. The father was Henry II of England, the son was Richard Cœur de Lion, then Duke of Aquitaine, who took opposite sides in a dispute between the brothers Bertrand and Constantin de Born over the right to the fortress. Today, Hautefort is one of the most important châteaux in Perigord, dominating the village below and the entire horizon.

The château was rebuilt in the 15th century, by the vicomtes d'Hautefort, with four towers at the corners. Two large cylindrical towers (*below*) remain at the south and south-east angles – the latter containing the chapel. Later, Charles, created marquis in 1614, decided to rebuild the château, but the work fell to his son, Jacques François, who built most of the present château, including a bridge (*left*), between 1640 and 1680. He was the brother of Marie de Hautefort, who inspired in Louis XIII a chaste but burning passion. Two masons directed the work, first the Perigordian, Nicolas Rambourg and second the Parisian, Jacques Maigret. The largely 17th-century corps-de-logis is flanked in the

cour d'honneur by two square towers with domes 'a l'imperiale' and containing fine stone staircases.

The Hauteforts retained the château till the Revolution. Subsequently it came as a dowry to the Baron de Dames, a survivor of Napoleon's Russian campaign. After the restoration of the monarchy, the baron served as minister of War and then Foreign Affairs, being named in 1828 the governor of the young duc de Bordeaux, the heir to the throne, who he followed into exile when the Bourbons were overthrown in 1830.

The baron's son, comte Maxence de Damas, retained Hautefort until his death in 1887. Then, in 1890, the château was sold to M. Artigues, and after a period of neglect was acquired by Baron Henry de Bastard, who undertook its restoration. On August 31, 1968, a savage fire gutted the château. The baron's widow, Simone David Weill, restored the house, only to see it burn again as a result of a cigarette dropped by a guest. A second restoration is now complete.

Evans's photographs are therefore an important record of the magnificent 17th-century boiseries. He conveys the imposing scale of the grande salle (*above*) with its stupendous columned chimneypiece (detail. *opposite*). Large two-tier chimneypieces

were, of course, a feature of French château from the 16th century. Here, with typical baroque éclat, the division into upper and lower zones melts away and the whole composition reaches a dramatic climax in the superb sculptured pediment of immense robustness. Instead of the usual cornice, the boiseries around the room have a full classical entablature complete with richly carved frieze. The rich decorative treatment was probably inspired by the engravings of Daniel Marot.

Evans's pictures of Hautefort were published in *Country Life* on January 6, 1917, with an article by W.H. Ward. He wrote "of all the castles of France, and they are reckoned by the thousand, not many are more arresting to the eye and imagination then lordly Hautefort, proudly planted on its limestone bastion, and dominating the waving woods of Born, the rich, populous hill-country of the Corrèze". The spur on which it stood – commanding the meeting point of several valleys – was, he observed, "the site beloved of the medieval sparrowhawk for his eerie – as well adapted for display as for defence". The splendid 17th-century interiors appealed less: "the clumsiness of the carved figures shows that a sculptor equal in merit to the designer was not forthcoming in this remote province".

CHAPTER TWENTY ONE

LANDIFER

The photographs taken by Evans pose an intriguing puzzle. Here is an apparently Renaissance house in such pristine condition it might be a 19th-century creation. Yet many details point to an earlier date: the small doors (19th-century owners tended to prefer porte-cocheres), the widely spaced, rather irregular windows, the numerous gun loops, and the fact that the main rooms appear to be on the upper floors. The explanation is simple: a Renaissance château was extensively restored and doubled in size around 1900, shortly before Evans arrived. Old engravings show a rectangular château with four large circular towers at the corners; the new extension, doubling it in size, was built backing onto the Renaissance house. Two corner towers (one shown *opposite*) were retained, resulting in the unusual flank with three towers (*below*). Nothing is known about the construction of the château, but it appears to date from the second quarter of the 16th century. Landifer stands a few kilometres south of the town of Baugé, a little way to the left of the road running north from Angers. It belonged in the 16th century to the family of Mareil, whose arms are sculpted over a chimneypiece inside. The position of

the Renaissance staircase is evident in the differing heights of the windows over the front door.

The château has the vertical linking of the windows characteristic of the Renaissance in the Loire Valley, but the classical detail is more carefully grammatical than in the early years of the 16th century. The pilasters are plain, not panelled in the Italian fashion. The richly carved dormers show no trace of Flamboyant Gothic and carry scrolls instead of flying buttresses. The huge soaring chimneys echo those at Chambord, but are still more monumental – these, like the dormers, have the curious detail of a pair of scrolls supporting the bottom like bookends. Though the towers remain as a reminder of the medieval château-fort, the machicoulis have been transformed into a richly carved bracket cornice. More puzzling are the gun-loops flanking the windows and encircling the towers – possibly a late introduction, dating from the Religious Wars of 1565-70.

Evans, as usual, photographs the château at an angle and in steep perspective (*above*) to add drama to the silhouette. He appears to have waited for a moment when the sunlight was virtually off the two main fronts and striking the sides of the dormers. Inside, Evans photographed a tapestry-hung saloon (*right*), dominated by a massive, full-height stone chimneypiece – very much like a medieval hooded fireplace, but classical in detail and inset with a large carving in low relief.

CHAPTER TWENTY TWO

LONRAI

Lonrai is the counterpart of what in England is called 'Wrennaissance', or Queen Anne Revival. It is an imposing Normandy château, five kilometres from Alençon, known for its stables and a large park of 180 hectares. The house is built in a Louis XIII style, overlaid with elements of Louis XVI such as the shallow portico of banded colonnades, which evokes neo-classical architects like Soufflot.

The layout is perfectly symmetrical: the château stands on a rectangular island in a rectangular moat with edges as straight as a rule. The bridge is in line with the steps leading up to the front door, so it is intriguing that all Evans's photographs are off-axis. He systematically avoids the head-on view: with the entrance front (*below*) he chooses a steep angle that gives quite a degree of distortion, but includes the whole of the newly planted parterre de broideries in the foreground. Another view (*left*) is taken at an angle to show the elegant arch of the stone bridge across the moat.

Evans's love of dramatically steep perspective stands out in his view of the back of the house. Here, the basement hidden at

the front by the raised forecourt, is revealed full height in the form of a graceful arcade with projecting loggias at either end (*above*). Part of the beauty of the design is the way the mirror-smooth water is almost on a level with the stone paths on either side, with a glimpse of mature planting in the English-style park at the end (*detail, right*). Inside, Evans photographed a beautiful neo-classical saloon with painted boiseries (*opposite*) – possibly rescued from an hotel privée in Paris demolished during Hausmann's rebuilding of the capital.

Two other points are worth noting. First, most but not all of the shutters on the front of the château are closed – nearly all owners would probably want to see them open, so it may be that the family was away. Second, though the sun was out Evans chose a moment when it was off both of the two main elevations he photographed.

In previous centuries, the estate had passed from the families of Silly and Goyon-Matignon to Colbert-Seignelay and Montmorency-Luxembourg. In 1892 it was acquired by the comtes de Marois, whose property it remains.

CHAPTER TWENTY THREE

MAINTENON

One of Evans's greatest talents was to convey the three-dimensional element of architecture. For this reason he rarely photographed his French châteaux head-on. When he did, as in the courtyard at Maintenon (*left*) he chose viewpoints that would reveal modelling to the maximum. By standing in front of the octagonal tower, rather than the archway, he gives a glimpse of the short façade to the left of the arch and the remarkable balustraded chimneystack beside it. The viewpoint also shows how strongly the three pointed roofs stand one in front of the other.

Evans liked buildings to dominate his pictures and had a penchant for bold diagonals as pronounced as any Italian baroque painter. At Maintenon this is seen in his view of the château from the canal (*below*), in the detail of the dormer windows (*page 127, bottom right*), and in the astonishing view of the great aqueduct (*pages 128-9*), where the perspective is almost as steep as in 1930s travel posters of ocean liners and express trains.

Maintenon has grown – and shrunk – through the centuries, but the changes have always respected the medieval courtyard

plan. First came a square donjon or keep in stone, of the 13th century. This forms one of the corners; the three others are marked by rather later round towers in brick (*detail page 129, bottom right*). Jean Cottereau, trésorier des Finances under Louis XII and François I, bought the estate in 1505. He retained the towers and keep, but rebuilt two sides of the quadrangle with a corps-de-logis on one side and a returning wing on the other. Inside, handsome ceilings of this date survive.

In 1526, Jean Cottereau's daughter married Jacques d'Angennes, seigneur of Rambouillet. The Angennes retained the property until the beginning of the 17th century, when it passed to the marquis de Villeray from whom Louis XIV bought it to present to Françoise d'Aubigné, who he married secretly in 1684. She entered history as Madame de Maintenon, and for her Maintenon was raised to a Marquesate.

Madame de Maintenon built a facing wing in the cour d'honneur. She also rearranged the apartments, the best preserved being an anti-chamber of gilt leather. In addition, the wall enclosing the fourth side was demolished to open up a dramatic view over the gardens (*above*). At the same time, Le Nôtre canalised the river Eure, extending the moats to create an island

parterre and continuing the axis of the château in a canal.

The vista is closed by the astonishing aqueduct of heroic, indeed Roman, proportions (*left*). This was not the ruin it appears today, but part of an extraordinary project masterminded by the great military engineer Vauban and intended to carry the waters of the Eure to Versailles. Theodore Cook angrily observed: "Whole regiments of infantry who were not wanted at the front...laboured at this aqueduct, the mortality being so great among them that cartloads of dead and dying had to be carried away every night...a more striking monument of fruitless and insensate recklessness does not exist in Europe."

Following reverses on the battlefield towards the end of Louis XIV's reign, the project was abandoned, but not before leaving Maintenon with the grandest garden folly in France. Finally Madame de Maintenon linked the corps-de-logis to the church of Saint Nicholas by a long gallery.

In 1698 Madame de Maintenon generously gave the château to her niece on the occasion of her marriage to the duc d'Ayen, son of the duc de Noailles. It remained the property of the Noailles for two and a half centuries and was subsequently restored in the 19th century.

CHAPTER TWENTY FOUR

MEILLANT

Meillant represents medieval romantic fantasy in its final, most exuberant flowering. The medieval love of pageantry and display, the delight in the trappings of warfare and chivalry, even though defence against assault was no longer the primary aim, are everywhere manifest in a wealth of bannerets, fleurs-de-lys and coats of arms (as in the doorway, *opposite*). Rarely has the plumber's art been carried to such heights: crocketed finials, weathervanes, and ornamental cresting are exquisitely worked in lead in awe-inspiring profusion.

No less remarkable is the stone carving. Dormers carry precarious superstructures so filigree that they defy the nature of the material (*page 132, top left*). Openwork balustrades and a profusion of gargoyles show the full vocabulary of Flamboyant Gothic in a display of frenzied virtuosity (*pages 134-5, and 137*). Amidst all this are the first soundings of the Renaissance: shellback niches, columns, ovolo mouldings and a dome and a cupola, interspersed with Gothic in a manner as unselfconscious as it is ungrammatical.

A château belonging to the Charenton family is recorded in the 11th century; in 1233 the property passed to Louis I de Sancerre. Étienne de Sancerre, who died in 1308, rebuilt the château, and the imposing bare south wall of his enceinte (*page 131*) survives to this day. In plan the château was an irregular polygon – a continuous circuit of high walls and towers, only part of which survives.

At the end of the 14th century, the property passed by marriage to Jean de Bueil. His daughter and heiress Anne married Pierre d'Amboise, bringing Meillant to one of the great families of late medieval France. Pierre d'Amboise had seventeen children, while his son Jean had a further sixteen. The greatest of Pierre's children was Cardinal George I of Amboise (d.1510), first Minister of Louis XII. His brother Charles owned both Meillant and Chaumont on the Loire, and on his death both passed to his son Charles II d'Amboise. His career was brilliant, but short: at twenty he was Governor of Paris, and when Louis XII came to the throne he was created grand maître de la Maison du roi. He also led the French armies in Italy, becoming Governor of Milan.

Charles II's phrase, 'Milan a fait Meillant', is a tribute to both the splendour of his château and his rapacious use of the Italian revenues. The corps-de-logis at Meillant is dominated by the ornate octagonal Tour du Lion. The walls are emblazoned

like those at Chaumont with interlaced 'C's and flaming mountains (chaud mont), a form of armes parlantes. Above is a tier carved with niches containing figures of soldiers (*left*) – a trompe l'oeil motif doubtless inspired by the figures of servants leaning out of blind windows on the entrance front of the Maison Jacques Coeur in nearby Bourges. The twin-pinnacled Tour des Sarrasins beyond (*above*) is emblazoned with 'L's and fleurs-de-lys commemorating a visit of Louis XII, while in the centre is his emblem: the porcupine.

The purest Renaissance work was to be seen on an arcaded wing built before 1511, the year of the death of Charles II d'Amboise. This was later demolished. It is visible in a drawing of Meillant by Claude Chastillon. From this wing survive a series of medallions with portrait heads of Roman emperors in antique style, resited on the main staircase. These are of superb quality and clearly by an Italian hand.

Prosper Mérimeé, founding father of preservation in France, visited Meillant on his *Voyage en Auvergne* in 1838. "All the apartments have been altered on several occasions, and there is not one where the furnishing or the decoration dates from before the 18th century. Only the fireplaces, as large as a modern room, appear to date from the original construction: all are of an excessive simplicity" he wrote. That very year an ambitious restoration had begun, with the architect Louis Normand working for

Virginia de Sainte-Aldegonde, the duchesse of Mortemart, who had inherited Meillant from her uncle the duc de Charost.

Evans's photographs form an important record of the 1840s interiors, complementing Normand's drawings and a series of 1860s water-colours in the château. In the Salle des Cerfs are three enormous stags carved in wood, with collars bearing the arms of Louis XII and Anne of Brittany, who came to Meillant in 1505. The Tour de Sarrazins, where the king slept, also bears a lead porcupine and his initials.

The Saloon is dominated by a massive two-tier chimneypiece with a minstrels' gallery above the hearth (*page 132-3*). The panels of the gallery are painted with a series of historical scenes in the style *Troubadour*, representing the arrival of the Cardinal d'Amboise and other events in the Château's history. Evans's photographs show elaborate neo-Gothic furniture (*right*), close to pieces in the *Album Gothic de Meubles et Sièges* published in the contemporary *Journal de Garde Meuble*. Evans's photograph of the Saloon also shows distinctly Puginesque Gothic chandeliers. In the dining room (*above*) are elaborate Gothic-revival side-tables, as well as an unusual centre table with dragon legs, also probably inspired by a drawing by Pugin.

CHAPTER TWENTY FIVE

MONTIGNY-LE-GANELON

This is a striking example of the kind of evocative, ancestral house of very mixed date to which Evans was led by the *Annuaire des Châteaux*. It is not a great set-piece of any one period, but a palimpsest of the centuries. Mont Ignis, or mount of fire, evokes the fires which were lit to send signals in primitive times. The château occupies a commanding position on a ridge above the River Loir, looking out on the other side over a vast flat plain. The name Gannelon recalls the Abbot Wanelo, or Gannelon in the *Chanson de Roland*, who was treasurer of Saint-Martin de Tours and abbot of Saint-Avit-de-Châteaudun.

Rebuilt by Jean de Montigny at the end of the 12th century, the château belonged two centuries later to the comte de

Dunois, who ceded it to Louis de France, the future duc d'Orléans, who constructed the château of Pierrefonds and refortified Montigny. After the battle of Agincourt, the walls and towers were dismantled to prevent the English from using the château as a stronghold, but between 1475 and 1495 the château was reconstructed by Jacques de Renty.

Subsequently it has changed hands many times, passing from the family of Fromentières to Raynier, until finally acquired in 1831 by Adrien, duc de Montmorency-Laval, who embarked on a major restoration. In 1836, a year before his death, he received Madame Récamier at the château. He also filled in the ditches on the west side of the house to create a parc anglais, and added the Montmorency pavilion to house the portraits of the sovereigns he had served as ambassador. Adrien's son-in-law, the duc de Levis-Mirepoix, continued the restoration of the elevation above the Loir. The château today belongs to the vicomte and vicomtesse Gérard de Talhouet and is open to the public.

The façade overlooking the park (*page 139*) has remained substantially unchanged since the 16th century. On the right is the donjon, or Tour des Dames, almost bare of windows and with the machicoulis that once supported a defensive wall-walk visible under the eaves. On the left is the Tour d'Horloge, which takes its name from the large clock set in a tabernacle on the roof. Between the two towers is an arcade on two levels, already Renaissance in style, though the once-open arches have now been filled in.

Evans also photographed the narrow south front overlooking a formal flower garden (*page 138*), which, with its open shutters, suggests the part of the house where the family lived. No less intriguing is the east front over the Loir (*above left*), designed *c.*1836 by the architect Clement Parent. This is a picturesque composition of turrets, dormers and bartizans, which on closer inspection is perfectly symmetrical around the central pavilion – with the exception of the lower wing on the right. In character it corresponds to Scottish houses of the 1830s, which have very much the same fairy-tale silhouette of slender pepper-pot towers.

Evans was able to photograph two interiors: a 19th-century vaulted corridor, with elaborate blind cusping over the windows, and his favourite theme, the spiral stair (*opposite*), here with an elaborate fan vault with ribs spreading out much like the ribbons of a maypole.

MONTREUIL-BELLAY

Evans made an extensive record of this imposing château, amounting to 37 negatives. It is particularly valuable as a portrait of the 19th-century revivalist interior decoration, for while painted ceilings have survived, stencilled walls have tended to be repainted and furniture has been rearranged. Evans provides the tout ensemble and the evidence of a château that was very much lived in. This is manifest in the bric-a-brac in the grand salon (*page 145, top*), and the china jugs and washbowls in the bedrooms (*page 144*).

The present château stands in a large irregular enceinte of fifteen towers (*opposite and page 147*). Two of these form the entrance. Evans tended to favour close-up shots to panoramic ones, but here the enceinte and the groups of buildings

clustered on it are so complex that they are difficult to comprehend in a series of isolated views. Evans took the trouble to find the viewpoint (*page 146, top*) that best explains their relation to each other, soaring above the waters of the River Thouet.

Fulk Nerra, the warlike Count of Anjou, granted the fief to the Berlay family (later Bellay) in the 11th century. In 1217 the château passed to the comtesse de Melun, who reconstructed it – probably creating the present enceinte. In 1415 the domain passed by marriage to Jacques d'Harcourt. His son Guillaume remodelled the château, reducing the height of the towers so they would be suitable for artillery. A chapel, today the parish church, was added in Flamboyant style, as well as lodgings for the canons.

The château was confiscated during the Revolution and turned into a prison, serving for a while to incarcerate women suspected of loyalty to the crown. Two hundred and sixty were locked away: peasants, bourgeois and aristocrats. Many died from typhus before the survivors were liberated following the death of Robespierre. After this the château was used as a grain store, and the donjon demolished. Then in 1822 a M. Niveleau, a merchant from Saumur, acquired it and let it to tenants.

His daughter, inheriting from her brother in 1860, began restoration with the help of a pupil of Viollet-le-Duc, Joly-Leterme. She married an officer at Saumur, Alexandre de Grandmaison, and gradually bought back the grounds (detail, *page 143*) which had been lotted up. She died of a broken heart after the death of the third of her sons and left Montreuil to an enterprising nephew of her husband's, George Millin de Grandmaison, who was mayor of the town for sixteen years.

During the 1914-18 war the château served as a hospital for the wounded. Today it remains the property of the Grandmaison family and is regularly open to the public.

Evans, using only natural light, took a very atmospheric series of interiors, in many cases adding interest by choosing viewpoints that provided a glimpse of a room or staircase beyond (*right and page 145, bottom left*). As many of these rooms were quite dark – lit perhaps only by one or two windows with deep reveals, and with curtains and pelmets further reducing the light – it was inevitable there should be a certain amount of flare, both from direct and reflected light. Evans showed his mastery in controlling this, using artificial light to create a more natural look.

CHAPTER TWENTY SEVEN

NANTES

One of Evans's most dramatic architectural photographs (*opposite*) shows the Grand Logis at the château de Nantes. With a rising front to his camera he could easily have adjusted the lens to include the little pyramid roof at the top of the soaring Flamboyant Gothic façade (detail *below*). But Evans, like a baroque painter, wanted to extract maximum drama from steep perspective and foreshortening. The key was the stone bench in the bottom right of the picture. Continuing on beyond the gateway, this gives an immediate sense not only of scale but of depth and recession, as well as providing the strong diagonal, which Evans liked so much, picked up in the retreating façade of the logis beyond.

Unusually, Evans included two figures, again adding to the sense of scale. By these means Evans gives the viewer an intense sense of architecture's two main constituents: space and mass. A lens with a perspective corrector such as Evans used allows a photographer to ensure the verticals are parallel even in a very steep shot like this, so it is all the more interesting that he was prepared to accept a distinct inward lean on the pillar framing the archway – a solecism

well hidden in the general drama of the photograph.

Nantes is at once fortress and feudal or ducal seat. In French history it has an added fame or infamy from those who had been rightly or wrongly incarcerated in the château. Here in 1440 the monstrously depraved Gilles de Rais was condemned to death. Here Louis XIV arranged, in somewhat cowardly fashion, the arrest of Nicholas Fouquet, the builder of Vaux-le-Vicomte. Here the duchesse de Berry was imprisoned in 1832 after her dramatic arrest in a house nearby. Here too Henry IV signed the famous Edict of Nantes, in 1598, guaranteeing freedom of worship to Protestants.

The château was first the seat of the counts of Nantes and then of the dukes of Brittany. Guy de Thouars, regent of the Duchy, built the Tour Neuve in 1205 – now vanished. The present buildings date from 1466, when Francois II, last duke of Brittany, reconstructed the château to the design of Mathelin Rodier, author of the Cathedral of Nantes. With the intention of uniting Brittany to France, his daughter, Anne, was married at Langeais in 1491 to Charles VIII, and after his sudden death, to cement the alliance, to the new French King Louis XII, in 1499, in the chapel of the château at Nantes (destroyed in 1800).

The Grand Logis begun by Francois to the designs of Jean Perreal, was completed by Anne. As so often with Flamboyant Gothic, architectural enrichment is concentrated on the top of the building – like a crown. Evans photographed the magnificent row of dormers (*above and page 149*), each one subtly different from its neighbour in size, proportions and detail, and as richly treated as a series of bishops' seats in a cathedral. Immediately to the north-east is the somewhat lower and simpler Aisle du Grand Gouvernement, which was reconstructed in the 17th century.

During the Revolution the château remained a prison, but was also used as an arsenal, an explosion destroying the Tour des Espagnols, the chapel and nearby houses. Restored in 1861, the château was granted to the city in 1915 and today houses a series of museums.

While many photographers use a wide-angle lens to show the sheer extent of the walls encircling the château, Evans concentrated on a single corner (*opposite*), using glancing light and shadow to highlight the complex system of rounded and angled bastions designed to avoid any blind spots. He also hints at the proximity of the town across the deep dry moat.

CHAPTER TWENTY EIGHT

PIERREFONDS

Evans's talents as a photographer stand out with astonishing power in his majestic survey of Pierrefonds. He shows Viollet-le-Duc's extraordinary and controversial restoration at its best, doing justice to every aspect of the enterprise: the distant views, the palatial courtyard (*opposite*), the superb sculptural detail and the rich interiors.

Begun in 1392, Pierrefonds was both fortress and palace. Louis d'Orléans, its builder, was brother of Charles VI and vastly enriched by his marriage to Valentine Visconti of Milan. Being politically ambitious and on very bad terms with his uncle, the Duke of Burgundy, he decided to fortify his domains vigorously. Defensive works were carried out at Crépy-en-Valois, Vez, Béthisy, Forté-Milon and Montépilloy. At Pierrfonds, for reasons of speed, he chose to build on the site of an existing manor, rather than the 'Rocher' close by, where the first seigneurs of Pierrefonds had built their château in the 11th and 12th centuries. The work was put in charge of Jehan Lenoir, master of the King's works at Senlis.

In plan, it was a pentagon, with five massive towers at the corners and a further three along the middle of the sides. Soaring

above the forest of Compiègne (*right*) it has the aspect of a celestial city, with windows enough for a town rather than a castle. This is partly because, around the crown of the building, each element is redoubled, the towers having not one set of battlements but two. Along the walls, a lower covered wall-walk, supported on machicoulis, is surmounted by another storey en retraite, and above this is an open wall-walk behind battlements, connecting with all the covered wall-walks around the towers.

Louis d'Orléans was assassinated by Jean Sans Peur in 1407, but by this time Pierrefonds was almost complete. Alas the very value of Pierrefonds as a stronghold, even in the age of the musket and the canon ball, was to prove its undoing. It was occupied by the League, but retaken by royal troops in 1593. Then rebels seized it against Louis XIII, and this time it was savagely slighted: great vertical gashes were cut in its walls. What survived was not a noble or picturesque ruin but a viciously mutilated shell. Yet its interest remained sufficient for Napoleon I to buy it, for Louis-Phillippe to banquet here, and for Napoleon III to take a renewed concern because of its proximity to his great residence at Compiègne.

In 1857 Viollet-le-Duc had published a theoretical restoration of the château. The next year, responding to the Minister of the Imperial Household, he proposed restoring the donjon, but "leaving all the other parts of the château in their existing

state of ruin, save for two towers which could be useful to restore for accommodation".

Early in 1862 the Emperor took a new decision to reconstruct Pierrefonds as a complete Royal Residence. In 1863 more than a hundred workmen were on site, even on Sundays, provoking protests from the Bishop of Beauvais. In December 1863 the Emperor decided to furnish the château and demanded detailed proposals from Viollet-le-Duc. In 1865 and 1866 the buildings of the Salle des Gardes and the Salle des Preuses rose in the courtyard, as well as the kitchen and office wing. In 1866 the Emperor's great collection of antique arms and armour was installed in the Salle des Preuses. Yet despite the frantic pace of work, the château was not habitable at the outbreak of the Franco-Prussian War in 1870.

In June 1870, Viollet-le-Duc reported nearly 5 million francs had been spent, and a further 800,000 was needed to complete the windows and the roof. His idealistic approach to the restoration of old buildings will always be contentious: he believed not only in restoring a building to its original state, but to what its architects intended – or would in his view have intended. But Theodore Cook, writing for *Country Life*, was

firmly behind him: "The whole external shell of the great donjon in the courtyard was perfectly preserved, with the height of every storey clearly marked. The stonework for receiving the treads of various staircases was still nearly perfect. The framework of the original windows was found among the debris and was all replaced in its original positions. Even the slope of the roofs was often shown in the lines left upon adjacent towers and walls. Every possible indication of the original workmanship was preserved with the greatest reverence and used with the most careful accuracy. All new work was modelled on the inspiration of the old".

It is the last sentence which is of course contentious. But setting aside scrape and anti-scrape and judging Pierrefonds as a 19th-century creation, Viollet-le-Duc's knowledge and appreciation of Gothic is revealed to stunning effect by Evans. He shows the donjon (*page 152*), the gallery outside the lower hall (*pages 153 and 156*), the statue of Louis d'Orléans on the eastern staircase (*page 157*) and the upper hall (*above and right*). Pierrefonds, in its way, is as much a triumphant fusion of all the arts as Vaux-Le-Vicomte. Viollet-le-Duc's work is astonishingly robust. Evans's genius shows that his flair and invention never lapsed.

CHAPTER TWENTY NINE

LA ROCHEFOUCAULD

❧

Evans came to the seat of the La Rochefoucaulds when the grass was growing long in the courtyard (*opposite*). He captured it before the great square donjon, or keep, collapsed for want of maintenance (*page 164, top left*). His photographs show the château towering majestically above the river and the town (*pages 164-5*), together with the exquisite masonry of the courtyard arcades and the view opened up to the country when the north wing was added (*below*).

The château was founded in the 11th century by a seigneur named Foucauld. The keep, dating from the 12th century, recalls those at Loches and Beaugency, though its machicoulis and defensive covered wall-walk date from the 14th-century remodelling. In the 15th century Jean de La Rochefoucauld was chamberlain of Charles VII and Louis XI, while Francois I, baron de La Rochefoucauld, was councillor of Charles VIII and Louis XII, and godfather of François Premier.

His son, Francois II de La Rochefoucauld, succeeded his father in 1517 and married Anne de Polignac the following year. He began remodelling the château in a Renaissance style, purer and more severe than contemporary work on the Loire, in 1520.

Here are the plain rhythmic arcades of contemporary Italy, yet inside the vaulting is still Gothic with ribs, pendants and corbels (*left*). Italian too is the device of paired arches on the upper storey set above the larger arches below. Most striking of all is the parapet of surging pediments emblazoned with shells and alternating with boldly sculptural finials (*page 161*). The work has been attributed to Antoine Fontan, and was continued after François II's death in 1533 by his widow Anne de Polignac, reaching completion in 1538.

François III, a leading Protestant, met a bloody death at the Massacre of Saint Bartholemew in 1572. His son François IV died fighting for the future Henri IV in 1591. François V became a Catholic in 1610 and twelve years later received a dukedom. From this time date a number of internal alterations, such as the cabinet-des-bains, with wainscotting painted with flowers and landscapes. François VI is famous, above all, for his *maxims*.

In the 18th century the west wing was reconstructed after a fire in a plain classical manner, with blind arches on the ground floor and gently round-headed windows above.

The Liberal Louis-Alexandre de La Rochefoucauld – one of the first to ally himself with the third estate in 1789 – fell victim to the mob three years later at Gisors. His estates passed to François-Alexandre, best known for his fascinating description of life in England, where he came to learn the language in 1784. Soon after the outbreak of the Revolution he had emigrated first to England and then to the United States, returning under the Consulate to pioneer new agricultural methods.

Today the château remains the property of the ducs de La Rochefoucauld, and the great donjon has been restored. Evans, fascinated as always by spiral staircases, took a powerful view of the top of a stair in the château, showing how gothic forms had been transformed with classical detail (*page 163*). More than usual with Evans, his photographs, though artistically composed, connect up to form a complete record of every façade of the château, both from outside and within the courtyard.

CHAPTER THIRTY

LE ROCHER-
MEZANGERS

Evans captured this dreamlike château, perched on the edge of a large lake, when it still wore its Victorian mantle of ivy (*below*). The original buildings were constructed in the second half of the 15th century for the family of Bouillé. The masonry of this date is plain and shorn of detail, but the composition with its numerous painted towers is picturesque.

The wing to the left of the cour d'honneur (*opposite*) dates from *c.*1535 and was built for Francois de Bouille, then grand falconer of François I. This is a delightful example of early Renaissance – pure in some details, capricious in others. The arcade on the ground floor has flat, not rounded, arches: these spring from capitals that are more Romanesque than Renaissance. But the Ionic pilasters facing onto the courtyard between the arches carry a full classical entablature, with the

tall frieze often favoured in the early Renaissance. Typical for this date are the scrolls of acanthus terminating in *putti* and the roundels inset in the shafts of the pilasters (*detail, above*).

Above there is an intriguing rhythm of alternating wide and narrow windows, the cornice is stepped up and down in response and the dormers over the wide windows are still flanked by the flying buttresses typical of Flamboyant Gothic – though here the detail is classical. The small pane windows – quite rare in France – give added character. To the left – visible in the view across the lake (*page 167*) – is the chapel. The detailing of the glazing is also particularly striking in the windows between the twin towers flanking the entrance (*right*), the arches being filled with an unusual pretty fern pattern.

Evans's most beautiful photograph is of a long narrow canal flanked by a stately line of limes (*opposite*), which are one of the great beauties of this part of France. In the foreground is a very attractive, yet simple bridge, edged not by a balustrade but a row of simple bollards shaped like squashed chess pawns.

CHAPTER THIRTY ONE

VALENÇAY

Valençay, when Evans photographed it, was already a shrine to Talleyrand, greatest of all Foreign Ministers and the man who said that none who had not lived before 1789 could truly know "La douceur de la vie". Though substantially of Renaissance design and form, the character of Valençay is in considerable part neo-classical, with interiors that are strongly Empire in spirit. It was in 1805 that Napoleon persuaded Talleyrand to buy the domain from the family of Villemorien-Luçay. Here he gave magnificent receptions, and here the deposed King of Spain, Ferdinand VII, resided with his family in forced exile from 1808 to 1814. On his death Talleyrand left the estate to his great nephew (petit nephew) Louis de Talleyrand, who Charles X created Duc de Valençay. The château today remains the property of Talleyrand's descendants.

The fascination Talleyrand has always held for the English is evident in the original article Theodore Cook wrote on Valençay in *Country Life*. He quotes Queen Victoria's letter to the King of the Belgians in May 1838: "Old Talleyrand at last is dead. I hear he showed wonderful composure and firmness to the last. He was one of those people who I thought would never die."

Cooks ends in valedictory style praising the minister who served first Louis XVI, then the Revolution and Napoleon, and finally the restored monarchy "Talleyrand was always consistent, always devoid of all hypocrisy; he loved his country, he sought peace...if he had conspired, then the whole of France were with him in the conspiracy. If he 'deserted' a cause, that cause had already lost everything essential to its being. If he 'attacked the Church', he only realised that since a part of its enormous revenues (including his own income) was necessary to the rest of the nation, the inevitable operation had better be carried out justly and advisedly...If he did not believe in the divine right of kings, he laughed at the divine right of the mob. He loved greatness but never forgot himself'.

Characteristically, Cook says not a word about the history of the house or interiors, though Evans's photographs, with his usual observant eye, pick out the many facets of the château's development. He begins with views of the grand axial avenue (*above and page 176, top right*), showing plane trees which, thought already tall, still have to meet to form the stupendous overarching cathedral nave that leads up to Valencay today.

Evans captures the long walks of pleached limes (*page 171*)

and the parterres punctuated by carefully clipped topiary (*pages 172-3*). He was intrigued with the splendid wooden seats in the arcades (*page 177*), and he also shows the large cylindrical towers, fronted with pilasters, and very similar to Chambord. (Indeed, as originally conceived, Valençay was clearly intended to emulate, if not quite rival, Chambord itself in scale and grandeur. The huge rectangular enceinte surrounded by ditches, the powerful corner towers and the enormous donjon in the centre all vie with François Premier's great château.)

Evans uses a telescopic lens to capture the powerful detailing of the top of the rectangular entrance tower, dated 1599, on one of the dormers (*page 173, top right*), showing machicoulis strangely carved with acanthus. He shows the classical 1760s courtyard front with Ionic pilasters capped with urns looking strangely like egg cups (*right*). But he is best of all inside, in the large airy saloons and corridors, achieving a remarkable balance of light even when he is looking towards the windows (*page 176, below*). In one view, looking into a saloon (*above*), Evans used the strong diagonal of his cathedral interiors, photographing through an arch towards a chimney-piece and using the mirror over it to show the reflection back across the room.

Theodore Cook wrote: "There are few other châteaux which exercise so magnetic an attraction when seen from a distance. Built on a plateau dominating the surrounding forests, the

stately mass of Valençay is visible for miles around. Some critics have objected that the domed towers, which are its peculiar characteristic, are not in keeping with the ornate donjon, but the complete effect is superb." Valençay, Cook noted, was a fitting centre for an estate which, until the death of the late Duke, extended for fifty thousand acres, a large area even for England, but unparalleled in France.

A picture of life at Valençay emerges from the memoirs of Talleyrand's niece and companion of many years, the Duchess of Dino. Here, she wrote, there was no shadow of politics. "We had goodwill, hospitality, practical employment of our time... at Valençay Monsieur de Talleyrand and I appear at our best.

Life at Valençay was on the lines of small royal court, rather than a country house. There was a constant flow of visitors: a retinue of doctors, lawyers, tutors and agents. There were frequent entertainments by musicians and travelling groups of actors. The Duchess would read voraciously, write numerous letters, sketch and do needlework. She enjoyed the charades and private theatricals – less so than Talleyrand's constant games of whist. She would also ride and drive in the carriage through the woods and go the rounds of the village doing good works.

CHAPTER THIRTY TWO

VALLIERE

In 1894 the duc de Gramont built a large Renaissance château in the parc of Mortefontaine. Here were lakes and a jardin anglais laid out by Le Peletier de Mortefontaine in the 18th century, and further embellished by Joseph Bonaparte. One of the most beautiful parks in the Ile de France (*page 180, below*), Mortefontaine is south of Senlis, and only some seven kilometres from another great 18th-century garden illustrated here: Ermenonville.

The château, barely ten years old when Evans photographed it, is in the Loire Renaissance style with steep roofs and candlesnuffer towers at the corners (*below*). In the middle of the east front are boldly projecting half-octagonal pavilions, one self-evidently containing a staircase.

Much of the character of the château derives from the extraordinary steepness of the roofs, which rise higher than the conical rooftowers at the corners. While the towers carry the usual soaring finials, the ridge of the main roof is without the elaborate cresting found on so many châteaux built or restored in the 19th century. The result, particularly over the central

pavilion, is rather awkward. Below, the large awning over the outdoor staircase adds a perfect period touch.

Though the façades were strictly symmetrical in design, Evans adopted diagonal viewpoints which emphasised the romantic and picturesque aspects of the château. Most characteristic is his view of the side elevation (*right*), where he chose a lens that makes the building fill the picture, never mind that the top of the tower in the foreground disappears out of view. Evans liked to convey the sheer monumentality of architecture, and this viewpoint shows the strong modelling of the façade to maximum advantage. Evans did not take it in full sun, but waited for the moment when the light was just clipping along the front and highlighting the curve of the very steep roofs.

Inside, Evans photographed an elegant Empire saloon (*page 178*), using the mirror over the chimneypiece to reflect the panelling and leaving the door ajar to hint at what lies beyond. Another view (*opposite*) presents an intriguing vista through three rooms.

CHAPTER THIRTY THREE

VAUX-
LE-VICOMTE

Vaux-le-Vicomte has long been regarded as the most splendid château and garden in the whole of France, taking second place only to Versailles as a supreme expression of the Grand Siècle. The château is also the subject of much the best chapter in *Twenty Five Great Houses of France*, the folio volume in which Evans's photographs were published in 1915. For once Theodore Cook, who wrote most of the *Country Life* articles which accompanied Evans's photographs, tells the story of the creation of the house and gardens, rather than simply recounting the lives and deeds of those who lived there.

Today Vaux-le-Vicomte is usually illustrated with aerial photographs, which show the elaborate patterns of the parterres à la broderie to their best advantage. Evans, in contrast, restricted his viewpoints to eye-level (*pages 186-7*), or sometimes a little

lower, so his vistas over the garden have a character more akin to 18th-century engraved views, and, unusually for Evans, when they were published they were cropped top and bottom.

Evans's most memorable shots were of the magnificent entrance screen with its giant herms standing back-to-back (*page 182*), and he conveys the robustness of the architecture (*opposite*) and the extensive moats which emphasise its grandeur (*page 183*) He also made his most extensive record of an interior. Just as his great views of cathedral interiors are often taken at angles that powerfully hint at what lies beyond the bounds of the picture, so Evans at Vaux-le-Vicomte chose viewpoints that provided a glimpse from one room to another, making masterly use of the reflections in mirrors to expand the sense of space (*above right*).

The view from the Salle d'Eté cleverly juxtaposes the inside of an arch with the coved ceiling in the room beyond, while the mirror provides reflections of the decoration on the opposite wall in both rooms – underlining the remarkable unity and state of preservation of the interiors (*page 186, top left*). The view of the dining room is aligned on a bust in the room, beyond which provides a perfect visual punctuation mark (*above left*), and Evans has waited for a moment when light streamed in so that it offers

a highlight in what would otherwise be a very dark photograph.

Vaux suffered little at the Revolution, but fell into gradual abandon after 1847 with the suicide of the duc de Praslin. In 1875 the domaine had been acquired by Alfred Sommier, who had taken on the task of restoring the château to its former splendour. Evans shows how magnificently he had succeeded, though subsequently the parterres have been further elaborated with broderie patterns in gravel replacing plain lawns.

The story of the building of Vaux-le-Vicomte has been told many times. It was built for Nicholas Fouquet, the surintendent des Finances, whose meteoric rise to riches was to evoke the jealousy not only of Colbert but the young King Louis XIV himself. Begun in 1657 it was built at astonishing speed: it was roofed by the end of 1658, and the decoration of the interior was complete by the fête of 1661. Fouquet was concerned that no one should know how many millions were being spent. Cook quotes a letter Fouquet wrote to his agent saying Mazarin would shortly be making a visit: "send away the labourers and masons working on the large canal, so that only a few may be seen, and let them go to the farms of Peuily or Maison-rouge, or to Maincy".

Fouquet's achievement was to assemble a team of artists and

craftsmen who could create a house that was a total unified
work-of art in a way never before seen in France. Le Vau was his
architect, Le Brun his painter and decorator, Le Nôtre his garden
designer. In the King's apartment Le Vau, Le Brun and his coll-
aborators Guèrin and Thibault Poissant the sculptor, invented
the style to be used at Versailles, with stucco, gilding and painting orchestrated together to provide one striking overall effect.

On August 17, 1661 Fouquet entertained the King, the
Queen, Mlle de la Vallière and the whole court with a new com-
edy ballet by Molière, music by Lully and a spectacular fire-
works finale. Three weeks later Fouquet was arrested at Nantes
for alleged embezzlement. All his property was confiscated and
the furniture of Vaux sold to meet the claims of creditors. His
enemy, Colbert, took over his team of artists to work for the
King – Vaux-le-Vicomte was thus the precursor of Versailles.

Fouquet died in 1680, but in 1673 the domaine had been
restituted to his wife. It was sold in 1705 to the duc de Villars
when Fouquet's son Louis-Nicholas died childless. Vaux then
entered a second glorious era: the house was furnished and hung
with great battle scenes (which survive) Louis XV was received
in splendour in 1731, but after Villars death three years later the
château fell into decline again. In 1764 it was sold to the duc de
Praslin, from whose descendants Alfred Sommier purchased it
and restored it to the state in which Evans photographed it.

CHAPTER THIRTY FOUR

VERVAINE

This imposing château must have been almost new when Evans arrived. It stand just outside Alençon in Normandy, in the commune of Condé-sur-Sarthe, not far from Lonrai, another very recent château photographed by Evans. The style is very much Louis XIII revival, with the characteristic mix of brick and stone (*opposite*), but there is a strong element of English freestyle. Though classical, the château is far from exactly symmetrical; there is a definite system of counterpoint in the way the steep pyramid roofs are repeated at the left end of both ranges (*pages 190-1*). This is the character Evans sought to capture, rather than provide a full descriptive record of the exterior.

In the *Annuaire des Châteaux*, Verveine is listed as the property of A. Fould. It has the appearance of a magnate's house – a great financier or industrialist, intent on putting on an impressive show. While the detailing on the windows, for example, is somewhat repetitive, there are eyecatching flourishes such as the open loggia linking the two wings, and the unusually tall and fragile cupola over the corner staircase tower, complete with a little bell-shaped dome. Evans's photographs also show a

lake (*top*), with a conservatory in the distance, and the mix of specimen trees, both conifers and hardwoods planted quite close to the house, that is typical of the later 19th century.

Inside, the main rooms are handsomely fitted out. Evans shows a double saloon (*page 189*), with an open arch linking the two halves of the room and a remarkable carved overmantel with intriguing and somewhat dwarf-like figures in 17th-century costume carved in virtual full relief (detail *above*). It is the counterpart of a Teniers inn scene carved in stone. Other photographs show elaborate wainscotting, large tapestries and the full classical entablatures, rather than single cornices, fashionable towards 1900.

With Vervaine, Evans brought the story of the French château right up to date. Working on his own, choosing his own houses, he provided a record and, more than that, a portrait of the French château in all its richness, splendour and diversity in a way that no writer or historian could have begun to do.

ACKNOWLEDGEMENTS

My thanks are due first to Camilla Costello, *Country Life*'s photographic librarian, for all her help in making Evans's photographs available. An excellent catalogue, listing all Evans's negatives at *Country Life*, was prepared by Paulette Barton and is available at the library, where Olive Waller and Joyce Warren have provided further help. New prints were made from Evans's negatives specially for this book by A.C. Cooper Ltd, and Kenneth Carroll and his assistant Roy Davison, of Carroll Associates, have played a crucial role in the shaping of the entire book. Alex Starkey, for many years *Country Life*'s Staff Photographer, gave me many useful tips and insights. *Country Life*'s editor Clive Aslett and his colleagues John Cornforth, Giles Worsley and Michael Hall have all had an important role in fostering the library and setting this series in motion. The never-failing enthusiasm of John Harris spurred me in my researches.
In France, I had vital leads from Edith de Richemont, Jean-Pierre Babelon, François Bercy, Vincent Bouvet and the tourist offices at Cantal and Puy-de-Domes.
My abundant thanks are also due to Judith More, Larraine Shamwana and Nina Sharman at Reed Consumer Books, but above all to John Wainwright who has shouldered the entire task of piloting the text towards publication with an abundance of patience, care and goodwill.

INDEX
Page numbers in italic refer to the illustrations